/kom'plisit/

Mildred Inez Lewis

BROADWAY PLAY PUBLISHING INC
New York
www.broadwayplaypublishing.com
info@broadwayplaypublishing.com

/kom'plisit/

© Copyright 2022 Mildred Inez Lewis

Cover art by Jaimyon Parker

First edition: October 2022
I S B N: 978-0-88145-951-7

Book design: Marie Donovan
Page make-up: Adobe InDesign
Typeface: Palatino

CHARACTERS

(in order of appearance)

AMANDA STIRLING, *40s, white, Executive Associate of JayVision Investments. Who knows what that means, but she runs the place. Working class Minnesota to Manhattan's Upper East Side.* JAY's *former lover, now close friend and procurer.*

JAY LITTLETON, *mid to late 50s, white, the founder, CEO and Chairman of JayVision. California working class roots, remade as Ralph Lauren. Silver fox. Doesn't have to look like an Olympian, but has to act like one.*

KESHA JONES, *late 20s, white, JayVision's top portfolio manager. From upstate New York, homely, earnest, butch. The stress from work has thinned her hair.*

GOLDIE ABDELLA, *early 20s, Indian American, tech geek moving into portfolio management. Perky, very Midwestern and modest.*

VIK ABDELLA, *50s, Indian,* GOLDIE's *father. A faded, beaten man, who wears the mask of a Republican glad-hander.*

REAGAN CLARK, *30s, African American, JayVision general counsel. Always done up. HBCU undergrad, Ivy League grad.*

WOMAN 1, 2, *and* 3, *offstage or pre-recorded voices. Doubled by* GOLDIE, REAGAN *and* KESHA.

SETTING

Executive Office, JayVision Investments.

*A lush, sensual penthouse office on the Upper East Side.
It is decorated with a surfing motif. A quiver of surfboards
stands near the entrance. There is a small sandbox, and an
unseen rooftop swimming pool. A large, gleaming JayVision
Investments sign hangs from the ceiling. A ultra-high
tech screen dominates one wall. There are other screens
throughout the office: electronic picture frames, consoles.*

*There are also hidden cameras everywhere, unseen, but
occasionally heard.*

*Production note: The monitors sometimes address the
characters. Other times, the audience.*

ACT ONE

Scene 1

*(In darkness, the monitors turn on. Fragmented, headless images of women, later revealed to be our cast [*GOLDIE, REAGAN, *and* KESHA*] are shown cleaning up the office. Water, waste, blood?)*

JAY: *(OS)* I like to watch. *(Whispers)* And...

(The WOMEN *speak as they clean, but we don't see their faces.)*

WOMAN 1: *(On screen)* Don't be alone with him.

WOMAN 2: *(On screen)* Watch your back.

(The screens go black.)

WOMEN *(OS. Whispers)* Help.

(The monitors flicker back on.)

WOMAN 2: *(On screen)* Lie.

WOMAN 1: *(On screen)* Scream, flatter. Beg.

WOMEN: *(On screen)* Fight. Do whatever you have to, but just...don't.

WOMAN 2: *(On screen)* His tell is—

WOMAN 1: *(On screen)* There are too many tells.

WOMAN 2: *(On screen)* They keep changing. You can't calculate fast enough to keep up.

WOMAN 1: *(On screen)* Even if you could, would your own distractions and illusions blind you?

WOMAN 3: *(On screen)* Beat it into your head that he's not your father.

WOMAN 2: *(On screen)* He's not invincible. Every snare needs cooperation from its prey.

WOMAN 1: *(On screen)* Don't be next. Leap over every sidewalk crack. Because if you get it wrong, it's going to be your own stupid fault.

WOMAN 2: *(On screen)* Then everyone. And I mean everyone, will turn on you.

WOMEN: *(On screen. Whispers even softer)* If I'd been smarter, if I'd, if, if, if…

(AMANDA enters as lights rise. She wears a sun dress over a stylish one-piece swim suit, heels and a straw hat. She swings a parasol.)

AMANDA: Stop.

(The "If" whispers grow louder. AMANDA talks over them until they stop.)

AMANDA: Who needs your warnings? Weak women rely on whisper networks. Tell me one time they made things right. Losers lose. Things can always get worse. There's no bottom. It's a dog eat dog world. You either play the game or the game plays you.

(JAY runs to the center of the office with his board and steps on a low table to "surf". He wears a wet suit with a bulge that dares you to notice.)

(Like Apollo, the sun god, a light beams from his bulge. It hits AMANDA who basks in its warmth. She rubs her arms as her skin starts to burn.)

AMANDA: The sun makes my skin peel. That makes me want it more. *(Laughs)* Why are we like this? Why do we crave the things that want to destroy us? To be consumed by them?

(AMANDA *raises her parasol to protect herself from the light and approaches* JAY. *He looks past her.*)

JAY: Surf's up!

AMANDA: Every woman has a superpower. When a straight man doesn't want to fuck you anymore, you turn invisible. If you don't want to fuck him, you start having options. But where do you find the strength to leave and never come back? (*Beat*) I need a swim. (*She closes the parasol and turns to leave.*) There's a pool upstairs. Jay insisted. Perks of the job.

(*The elevator dings.* AMANDA *gets on and exits.* JAY *sniffs in her direction.*)

JAY: Department store brand. Tacky. You can have a three thousand dollar outfit on and give yourself away by your scent. Or your shoes. Rich people made my mother laugh. "Scruffy as hell, with six hundred dollar loafers on." Us poor boys? If we make it, it's got to be designer all the way. (*He takes in the office.*) I mean take a look at my kingdom. My kids can walk in here holding their heads up. I don't know how I made it happen, but damn I'm good. Succeed and they'll call you a prince among men.

(JAY *cups his hand in the golden light beam and shines the light on the audience.*)

JAY: Bask. (*He unzips his wet suit dangerously low.*) Tell me I don't make you smile. I'm ridiculous. Who isn't? It's all a game. What's the point in taking anything seriously? (*He pats his bulge, then stares at the audience.*) Ah! Caught you looking. It's okay. It's good, natural. Things only go bad when we repress our needs. Are you repelled? Intrigued? Wet? (*He looks around and sniffs.)* To the pool. Can't leave Mandy alone with her thoughts.

(JAY *Baywatch runs to the elevator with his surfboard. Elevator dings. Lights out.)*

(End Scene)

Scene 2

(The monitors turn on displaying psychedelic surfing screensavers. Lights rise.)

(GOLDIE *enters with her father* VIK. *She wears a conservative "first day" outfit. He is in a frayed suit with an American flag lapel. He carries a large shopping bag.)*

GOLDIE: This is it.

(VIK *spots the surfboards.)*

VIK: A grown man, the leader of a concern of this size, keeps playthings at his place of business?

GOLDIE: You've always said success deserves reward.

VIK: Fun. When the best I can manage with a degree from—

(GOLDIE *pats* VIK's *hand.)*

GOLDIE: It's definitely not your typical hedge fund. But I think it might be fun.

VIK: Fun. You're sure these people are sponsoring you?

GOLDIE: It's a done deal. Don't worry pita.

VIK: I'm ashamed you have to carry this burden.

(VIK *gives* GOLDIE *the shopping bag.)*

VIK: A care package from your mother and I. We know you gave us most of the signing bonus. You're a good daughter.

(VIK *takes* GOLDIE's *hands.)*

VIK: You were looking for work for such a long time.

GOLDIE: You know how hard I tried. I sent out dozens of resumes. I blame—

VIK: No! I will not tolerate any child of mine making excuses. Take responsibility for your failures. You foolishly thought that award meant you'd have the world at your feet.

GOLDIE: I think we all did.

VIK: Then we were all stupid. No, I blame myself. Your mother and I had no connections here. If we'd stayed in Delhi—

GOLDIE: If we'd stayed in Delhi, we'd have nothing. Look at what happened to the mosque.

VIK: Do these people know you're Muslim? You don't tell them anything. Not a word. Do you understand?

GOLDIE: Things like that don't matter here. At least not as much.

(VIK *grabs* GOLDIE's *arm.*)

VIK: Your mother and I sacrificed to give you a better life. Don't throw that away. Keep your head down.

(AMANDA *enters.* GOLDIE *jumps up.*)

GOLDIE: Ms Stirling!

AMANDA: Amanda. Who's this?

GOLDIE: My dad. He came for my first day.

VIK: I was just leaving, ma'am.

GOLDIE: I should've asked—

AMANDA: You thought he'd be gone before I got here. (*To* VIK) All the way from upstate, dad.

VIK: I can't thank you enough for what you're doing for my girl.

AMANDA: I wish my father'd done the same thing. It was a different time. All is forgiven. Our girl is a rising star.

VIK: To hear you say that is... Sorry I talk too much. My wife is always saying this.

AMANDA: In the future, this is a restricted area. There are sensitive documents. We can't take a chance—

VIK: Understood. It won't happen again. You have my word. *(He flees.)*

AMANDA: He's quick on his feet.

GOLDIE: I'm mortified.

AMANDA: It's okay. I was a daddy's girl, too.

GOLDIE: Then I'm in good hands.

AMANDA: You are. What kind of work does he do?

GOLDIE: He was driving a cab, but quit to start a newsletter, the *Upstate India Times*.

AMANDA: How much volume does that do?

GOLDIE: My mom and I keep it afloat.

AMANDA: Then it's not a business. It's a charity.

GOLDIE: We couldn't crush his dreams.

AMANDA: As long as you realize that won't fly here. We don't do charity.

(GOLDIE nods.)

AMANDA: Kesha should be here any minute. Then we're right into the Monday meeting.

GOLDIE: Was I supposed to have something prepared?

AMANDA: How could you? Relax. It's just a quick check-in.

(KESHA enters.)

AMANDA: Behold, the heiress apparent.

KESHA: Thanks, boss. Hey it's Goldie, right? Welcome.

(GOLDIE *and* KESHA *shake hands.*)

KESHA: Good grip.

GOLDIE: Nice to meet you.

AMANDA: Let's get started.

KESHA: Shouldn't we wait for Reagan? It's not eight yet.

AMANDA: On time is late. She should be here already. HR's not coming so we can go.

KESHA: *(To* GOLDIE*)* Good. HR's out of control.

(GOLDIE *raises an eyebrow.*)

AMANDA: They're supposed to be spying for us, not telling us what to do.

(REAGAN *enters.*)

REAGAN: You've already started?

AMANDA: It's two minutes to eight. You know the old saying. If you're on time, you're late.

REAGAN: I'll take that under advisement. Who's this?

KESHA: This is Goldie.

REAGAN: Who or what is a Goldie?

AMANDA: Meow!

KESHA: She's taking over for Allison.

AMANDA: We brought her over from Merrill, upstate. She won the Banker's Award for that new modelling app.

REAGAN: I heard about that.

GOLDIE: You know it?

REAGAN: I do. Reagan Clark, JayVision General Counsel.

GOLDIE: I saw your bio on the website. Super impressive. I'm from a state school.

AMANDA: So what? I barely graduated from secretarial college.

GOLDIE: Really?

AMANDA: That's why I love the Street. The only thing that matters is what you can do.

KESHA: As long as you're able bodied and attractive.

REAGAN: Now that you mention it I've never seen a really homely person on the Street. Can't comment on the able bodied. That might be actionable.

AMANDA: Wall Street's crawling with Ivy League lawyers. Those schools polish away your drive. *(She side-eyes REAGAN.)* Upstarts make things happen.

GOLDIE: That makes me feel like I have a chance. No disrespect, Ms Reagan.

REAGAN: None taken. Everyone poops on lawyers until they dig themselves back into a deep enough hole.

KESHA: Ladies. Play nice. *(Points)* The new girl?

GOLDIE: Don't mind me. This is informative.

REAGAN: Sharper than she looks.

GOLDIE: It's an honor to join a team with so many spirited, accomplished women.

AMANDA: Women run this joint.

REAGAN: Untrue, we administer it. We're moons to Jay's sun.

AMANDA: The moon shifts the tides. That's power.

KESHA: Truth.

AMANDA: Alright, Jay's headed to Reykjavik next week. If he closes this, we'll be doing business directly with Iceland. There's no bigger piggy bank than a nation. It'll take us to a whole other level.

KESHA: *(To* GOLDIE*)* The long searched for foothold into Europe.

AMANDA: Jay and I dreamed of this from the beginning. I still have family in London. This move just makes sense.

REAGAN: Let's get excited after the ink dries.

AMANDA: Lawyerly caution didn't get us to the table. Balls did. You want your wins elegant. I'll take them any way we can get them.

REAGAN: My job's to advise you of the monsters under the bed and around the corner.

GOLDIE: I have a stupid question.

AMANDA: Probably. *(To* GOLDIE*)* Don't invite criticism. Shoot.

GOLDIE: Iceland's not in the EU so why start there? Why not just go for it?

KESHA: I see we can't slip anything past her.

AMANDA: It's only a step away.

GOLDIE: With JayVision's track record, Europe shouldn't be hard to crack. Clients should be coming to you.

AMANDA: We pay a price for being non-traditional.

GOLDIE: You'd hope that people would be open to female teams by now.

REAGAN: I'm not sure that explains it.

AMANDA: No telling tales out of school.

REAGAN: I make sure not to know any tales unless I'm forced to litigate them.

KESHA: *(To* GOLDIE*)* Can you write an algorithm to fix the two of them?

AMANDA: I'd like to see her try. Status reports?

REAGAN: Everything's in place on my end. Local counsel's instructed, fired up and ready to go.

AMANDA: I've added him presenting a gift to Haf on the last day. It's an Icelandic save the oceans deal.

REAGAN: Nice touch.

GOLDIE: It's definitely on brand.

AMANDA: Jay's got to come back with a win, either way. Stay glued to your phones until he's back. Bathroom, gym, during sex, at the dentist. In fact, cancel the dentist. If Jay needs us, we need to be on it. *(To* GOLDIE*)* I'm onboarding you, too.

GOLDIE: I'm not sure how I could help, but if you think I can be helpful.

AMANDA: Orders come straight from Jay.

GOLDIE: Mr Littleton knows who I am?

AMANDA: No one walks through those doors without him knowing.

*(*JAY *appears on the overheard monitor.* GOLDIE *jumps up, then isn't sure what to do: salute, bow?)*

JAY: I believe that's my cue. Welcome aboard, Goldie! Jay here.

GOLDIE: Sir!

*(*AMANDA *turns off the monitor, then displays the remote.)*

AMANDA: Relax, it was pre-recorded.

*(*AMANDA *and* KESHA *howl with laughter.* REAGAN *cracks a smile.)*

KESHA: The look on your face.

AMANDA: Priceless.

(KESHA *high fives* AMANDA.)

REAGAN: Take it in stride. They put me through it too. For some reason, they love to play these little games.

AMANDA: How can we bond without a good, solid hazing?

GOLDIE: I think I like this. My previous office was a little quiet.

AMANDA: You'll catch on. *(To* KESHA*)* You forgot to order a masseuse for the yacht.

KESHA: Is that absolutely necessary?

AMANDA: Did you think I wouldn't notice? Jay needs his outlets.

KESHA: Some boredom might not be the worse thing.

AMANDA: Do you want us to risk it?

GOLDIE: Everyone deserves to let off steam.

KESHA: Maybe you shouldn't be so sure about that.

AMANDA: Everyone here stands to benefit greatly if this goes through. One per cent of any deal you close. That's on top of commission.

GOLDIE: Would I be eligible? I mean in the future.

AMANDA: Once you earn your stripes, I don't see why not.

GOLDIE: It would mean everything.

KESHA: *(To* GOLDIE*)* Going from software engineer to deal maker's going to be awesome. Trust me.

AMANDA: You're in too, Reagan. Jay insisted on it.

REAGAN: Which means you were opposed.

AMANDA: I didn't oppose you. I thought participation should be restricted to employees who bring in business. Line employees, not staff.

REAGAN: None of this would be happening without me. I'm the only one with European experience and connections.

AMANDA: All hail, Yale. Iceland was my idea.

REAGAN: And a good one. I'll be sure to recognize your contribution during the negotiations.

KESHA: Well, who here doesn't want to be rich? Seeing no hands.

AMANDA: *(To* GOLDIE*)* Here's your first official duty. I'm tasking you with logistics confirmation.

REAGAN: It doesn't sound like I need to be here for this.

AMANDA: See? This is exactly what I mean.

REAGAN: I'm afraid I don't take your point.

AMANDA: Is that the attitude of someone who makes it rain? Or a professional ready to cut and run at the first sign of trouble.

REAGAN: Trouble or something else?

KESHA: Seriously you two. Let's take it down a notch.

(AMANDA *nods and strokes* KESHA*'s hair.)*

AMANDA: You're right. *(To* REAGAN*)* Sorry.

REAGAN: *(To* GOLDIE*)* Stop by later to sign your NDA.

GOLDIE: I signed it already.

REAGAN: That one was for the interviews.

KESHA: Trust me. You want to do this. It protects you and JayVision.

GOLDIE: Why would I need protection from my own firm?

REAGAN: You are new. I'll you later. *(Leaves)*

AMANDA: *(To* GOLDIE*)* Here's your assignment. It won't take any time at all. Make sure Jay's checked into the penthouse at every hotel. It gives us the most privacy on his itinerary. And confirm his yacht reservations.

GOLDIE: I'm sorry. You want me to call Mr Littleton's hotels?

KESHA: Allison never got around to it, then it fell to me. And I've got too much on my plate.

AMANDA: It needs to be done stat.

(KESHA *unsuccessfully tries to silently warn* GOLDIE.)

GOLDIE: I don't mean to complain.

AMANDA: But?

GOLDIE: I know I just got here. I expect to do whatever's needed. But I was hired to integrate my app into JayVision's system and become a portfolio manager.

KESHA: And that's going to be amazing. Your stuff's cutting edge.

AMANDA: When we optimize things for Jay, it puts him in a zone. I've seen it a thousand times, but still can't explain it. Amazing opportunities come out of that head space.

(KESHA *raises her hand.*)

KESHA: Resident butch here.

GOLDIE: Okay.

KESHA: Jay's never once let a client punk me. One time we walked after a client called me a bull dyke. All during negotiations, this asshole kept pushing me.

AMANDA: That guy from the Crescent fund.

KESHA: Jay punched him in the throat on our way out. Leaving a very sweet six-figure fee on the table. Who does that?

AMANDA: He's not violent. That prick had been pushing and pushing. He had it coming.

REAGAN: Clearly the actions of a pacifist.

KESHA: So we don't mind doing these little things for him.

AMANDA: The get's way better than the give.

GOLDIE: I'm not above it. I just hope this type of task won't be a regular part of my duties.

KESHA: If he gets off on pretending we're some kind of harem, so what?

GOLDIE: Has he taught you how to get into that zone?

KESHA: It's not something you can learn.

GOLDIE: I'm a software engineer. I'm very wary of mystique. There must be a way to model what he does.

AMANDA: Better living through algorithms? Nothing beats the human touch.

GOLDIE: If we can model it, we could replicate it. Double its impact.

KESHA: When you see, you'll believe.

AMANDA: *(To* GOLDIE*)* I've gotta say I admire your spunk. Objecting to an assignment right out of the gate. *(She gives a laugh that's not quite a laugh.)*

GOLDIE: Of course it's no problem. Have MBA, can dial eight-hundred numbers.

AMANDA: There you go.

GOLDIE: Sorry, I don't know what I was thinking. My dad's always warning me not to natter on.

AMANDA: This time isn't just about JayVision. If this deal closes, Jay promised to give me my own shop in London. That gives each of you a chance to move up.

KESHA: You haven't mentioned London for a long time.

AMANDA: I'm going through the change so change has to happen. *(To* GOLDIE*)* I'll be back to take you to lunch. It's our first day tradition. Kesha, you coming with?

KESHA: I'm buried.

AMANDA: So be it. *(She leaves.)*

KESHA: She hadn't mentioned London for so long. I thought she'd forgotten about it.

GOLDIE: Should I be worried?

KESHA: I don't think so. She and Jay are tied at the hip. I don't think she really wants to go. It's a fantasy.

GOLDIE: I hope it doesn't happen. At least not any time soon. I've got a lot to learn from her.

KESHA: It's good to have someone my own age around.

GOLDIE: Likewise. I've mastered algorithms. I need help with people.

KESHA: I've got your back. Here.

*(*KESHA *hands* GOLDIE *a thick folder.)*

KESHA: The check off sheet's in the front. Log in, FAQs.

*(*GOLDIE *flips through the pages.)*

GOLDIE: Where should I set up?

KESHA: It's an open floor plan. Do you.

GOLDIE: Got it.

KESHA: When you call the hotel, don't give your name, rank and serial number. Just say you're calling from JayVision.

GOLDIE: Why?

KESHA: Amanda's great, but she doesn't always tell us everything.

GOLDIE: She doesn't have to. We report to her.

KESHA: When you're right, you're right.

(They begin working.)

GOLDIE: Kesha, the way that sounded. I guess I'm still a little rule follower. I hope you'll help me break out of it.

KESHA: If that's what you want.

GOLDIE: It is. I didn't mean any disrespect.

KESHA: We're checking things at the tail end. Who knows what happened during the in between? Allison used to preach: only vouch for what you know for sure, for sure.

GOLDIE: Smart. Why'd she leave?

KESHA: I never got a chance to ask her. On the Street, you get fired you walk the same day.

GOLDIE: She seems to be doing fine at the Fed. I saw a piece about her in the *Journal*. She praised Jay.

KESHA: Maybe she was always destined for public service. Me? I'm content to be a corporate shill.

GOLDIE: I've never heard anybody say it out loud. Me, too.

KESHA: Bet.

(They settle into work.)

GOLDIE: Hey Kesha? Thanks.

KESHA: Course. Buckle up. The ride can get wild.

(End Scene)

Scene 3

(A few days later. AMANDA and GOLDIE are working late. The monitors silently stream Iceland news.)

GOLDIE: I wonder what time it is in Reykjavik?

AMANDA: Almost three in the morning. What are you still doing here?

GOLDIE: Integrating the block chain into—

AMANDA: I call bullshit. Confess.

GOLDIE: I don't feel right leaving you here alone.

AMANDA: We don't compete to see who can stay the longest. If you're not doing your best work, go home.

GOLDIE: This is different. At Merrill—

AMANDA: Merrill's behind you. I'm giving you ten minutes, then we're both leaving. I'm only here because my husband took our girl chick to a Nets game. I didn't feel like going home to an empty house.

GOLDIE: What's her name?

AMANDA: Lotty, for my mother. She died when I was young. Lotty never met her obviously.

GOLDIE: Oh!

AMANDA: Don't. I'm over it.

GOLDIE: Sorry you missed a chance for a girl's night. Maybe another time.

AMANDA: I don't do girlfriends. I prefer men. They don't get catty.

GOLDIE: I'd be lost without my bff. I guess I got lucky.

AMANDA: If true, then yes you have. You have a boyfriend?

GOLDIE: No.

AMANDA: Do you want one?

GOLDIE: (Laughing) Does it matter? As soon as I got this job, my mom started running matrimonial ads.

AMANDA: What's that like? I can't imagine that kind of interference, care…

GOLDIE: Not the stereotype. Parents don't want your marriage to fail.

AMANDA: What are your parents? Hindu, Moslem?

GOLDIE: All Indians participate in this craziness. Anyway, your parents want you to be happy.

AMANDA: What if your parents aren't good?

GOLDIE: They still love you.

AMANDA: In a perfect world.

GOLDIE: Sometimes I forget how fortunate I am.

AMANDA: Easy to do.

GOLDIE: I'm not totally relying on my mom. Every once in a while, the bff and I hit Desi single parties.

AMANDA: Go it alone. Girlfriends are cock blockers.

(GOLDIE *is shocked.*)

AMANDA: You're wondering, do the offenses end with a potty mouth? If you're fragile honey, JayVision's not for you. We're breaking barriers. Sometimes that leaves collateral damage.

GOLDIE: Let me prove myself. I'll help you with whatever you're working on top of my assigned tasks. London, for instance. Throw it to me. I'll catch it.

AMANDA: I don't think anyone can help with London. The world around it keeps changing. Brexit? I definitely didn't see that coming. What next?

GOLDIE: Why London? If you don't mind my asking.

AMANDA: My dad worked on the exchange. He came from nothing, made a fortune, lost it. It's why we moved to the States. I want to give Lotty a London girlhood.

GOLDIE: You dad must be so proud of you.

AMANDA: He's dead. Suicide.

GOLDIE: Oh my god.

AMANDA: The best I can do is get our fortune back to where it was for Lotty.

GOLDIE: If anyone can, you can. You're the highest paid woman on the Street.

AMANDA: No thanks to the big firms. JayVision made me. That's why I give women like you a shot.

GOLDIE: And Allison?

AMANDA: Kesha, a bunch of others. Sometimes things work out. Sometimes they don't.

GOLDIE: I intend to do you proud.

AMANDA: You're going to do more for us than we're doing for you. That's how it works.

GOLDIE: I accept the terms.

AMANDA: You're brilliant. You're just not savvy or stylish enough to overcome that dark skin. You need cold, hard cash to rise.

GOLDIE: It sounds bad, but I know you're right.

AMANDA: Your parents have your love life taken care of. I've got your back here. You remind me of me. You might be a "nice" girl, but underneath I think JayVision's found itself a stone cold hustler.

GOLDIE: Busted. My secret plan is to outwork everyone.

AMANDA: Truths have been told. Now I own you.

GOLDIE: I think I want that.

AMANDA: Good, cause that's what you're getting.

(AMANDA *feels* GOLDIE's *arm.*)

AMANDA: Soft. You should be firm, like a young lioness.

GOLDIE: People here seem to work out way more than they do back home.

AMANDA: If you don't have time for the gym, there's a pool upstairs.

GOLDIE: I never learned how to swim. Immigrant parents.

AMANDA: Did they want you to die? Kids can drown in like a tablespoon of water.

GOLDIE: My mom researched sports with the best scholarships and came up with lacrosse. We trained off of YouTube. There was no time for much of anything else.

AMANDA: I'm enjoying learning more about you.

(AMANDA *rubs* GOLDIE's *back.*)

AMANDA: Everyone says touch has no place in the office. I disagree. Work's the most intimate space in our lives.

(GOLDIE *diplomatically pulls away.*)

AMANDA: You really want my mentorship?

GOLDIE: Yes.

AMANDA: Then some advice. That's a sweet outfit, but it's not going to cut it. You look like a little girl.

GOLDIE: Modesty's important to me.

AMANDA: Women live and die by the theology of pretty. Our bodies are weapons. Decide how you're going to use yours before someone else does.

GOLDIE: Maybe that's been your experience.

AMANDA: It takes more than a few waves of feminism crashing into the shore to make the sea change you think's already happened. Jay likes his girls pretty. Get a membership somewhere. Or use the pool upstairs. You can use my suit.

(AMANDA *touches* GOLDIE's *collar bone.*)

AMANDA: You're about my size.

(End Scene)

Scene 4

(After hours. AMANDA *types on her laptop.* JAY *starts cleaning a surfboard.)*

AMANDA: You're taking that one, too? It doesn't exactly scream sober, international businessman.

JAY: Good. That's not me. After all this time, I thought you understood. We make our own rules.

*(*AMANDA *snaps her laptop shut.)*

AMANDA: Okay, you're briefed. I hope you and Reagan have a wonderful time.

JAY: Is my Mandy jealous?

*(*JAY *touches* AMANDA's *shoulders. She shrugs him off.)*

AMANDA: In your dreams.

JAY: Or memories.

AMANDA: Don't you think it's time to start thinking before you say actionable things?

JAY: If I were you, I wouldn't be so quick to judge. Everything I've done, we did together.

AMANDA: Not everything. Besides, I've cleaned up my act.

JAY: Maybe. Come, make yourself useful.

*(*JAY *hands* AMANDA *a wax block. They wax opposite sides.)*

JAY: Gently. How's the new portfolio manager? Should I should take her under my wing?

AMANDA: I can't see how she'd have time. Her parents are trying to arrange her marriage.

JAY: Why'd you feel the need to say that?

AMANDA: Portfolio managers are the core of our business.

JAY: And? She doesn't need your protection. You're an integral part of this machine. You tell me. What danger could she be in? Should we alert HR?

AMANDA: You make it so damned easy for them.

JAY: Are we talking about Allison?

AMANDA: Among others.

JAY: Allison never took responsibility for her part in our misunderstanding.

AMANDA: Nice. From settlement to misunderstanding.

JAY: I don't know if I ever fully thanked you for all your help. One thing I'll say for you. You don't let abstract ideas about sisterhood stand in the way of what has to be done.

AMANDA: You put us in an incredibly bad situation. I'm still pissed about the way you handled the aftermath.

JAY: And you waited until now to tell me?

AMANDA: I should've—

JAY: That's right, you should've. Low blow to throw me under the bus now. For the record, whatever the bitch thought she saw, didn't rise to the level of criminality or the much in vogue, trauma.

AMANDA: It kept us in depositions for months. What's the opportunity cost for that?

JAY: What was she expecting, spying on me? Does she know how to operate Google? My reputation's all over the net.

AMANDA: Crisis management said to stay low. You refused to stay off social media.

JAY: Did you think I'd let goddamned consultants run our business? How many times have they been wrong? We prevailed because I took a stand. Last time I looked, we haven't been sanctioned. No one's in jail.

AMANDA: It cost us.

JAY: A couple of hundred thou. So what? That's not even a rounding error.

AMANDA: Reputational damage costs.

JAY: Thinking of London? The tabloids can be brutal. Your family—

AMANDA: I do not want to have this conversation.

JAY: Maybe you want Goldie for yourself.

AMANDA: Jesus Christ. It's her first real job on the Street.

JAY: That's not a "no".

AMANDA: William and I are very happy.

(JAY *snorts.*)

AMANDA: How's Jane? Whoops, Saskia.

(JAY *gives a broad smile.*)

JAY: Goldie might welcome my mentorship.

AMANDA: I need continuity in that spot. You gave me your word if Iceland went through, I could open a London shop. I can't do that without a solid, experienced team in place.

JAY: London…

AMANDA: I didn't know I still wanted it until I was talking to the new girl and heard myself say it out loud.

JAY: You can't leave. This place would fall apart.

AMANDA: If that's true, I'm a piss poor manager. Look, I would never lave you high and dry—

JAY: So what, low and moist?

AMANDA: Eventually we're both going to have to—

JAY: No! Raw garlic every day. Wheat grass shots.
Yoga, tennis, weights.
I might age, but I'm never going to die.

AMANDA: Do you hear how crazy that sounds?

JAY: Facts. Do you know how long I can keep it up? I'm
talking without pills of any kind. I can still get hard on
demand.

AMANDA: Enough.

JAY: Want to check?

(AMANDA *gives* JAY *a dirty look.*)

JAY: You haven't always been this delicate. You used to
like things a little dirty and rough.

AMANDA: You really want to know?

JAY: Goes without saying.

AMANDA: My baby's started to bleed. I didn't think it
would make a difference. There are certain thoughts I
can't have in my head anymore.

JAY: Lotty can't read your mind.

AMANDA: I'm not sure about that. Sometimes it feels
like she's trying to jump back inside me. She gets so
close she snatches my breath.

JAY: How sweet.

AMANDA: I know what it would do for her to live in
London.

JAY: Away from me? Away from what your father did?

AMANDA: She understands about the suicide.

JAY: The other thing. When he crossed the line with
you—

(AMANDA *shivers.* JAY *cradles her.*)

AMANDA: You promised to never bring up…

JAY: Shhh. You're over it, remember?

AMANDA: I'm over it. *(She starts to shake.)*

JAY: Hold your arm out.

(AMANDA *does. With great effort, she holds it still. He kisses her palm.*)

JAY: Just saying his name used to freak you out. See how much stronger you are?

(AMANDA *nods.*)

JAY: That's because of us, together. He's never going to hurt anybody again. Not you. Not anybody.

AMANDA: Not safe here.

JAY: I won't stand in your way, if you really want to go. I just don't know what the hell I'm supposed to tell people.

AMANDA: It wouldn't be right away.

JAY: The hell difference does that make? People expect Jordan *and* Pippen. If we break up, what is JayVision?

AMANDA: Teams have to rebuild. Goldie…

JAY: I don't care how smart she is. She's green as grass. We don't know if she'll flow with how we work.

AMANDA: Maybe things can work differently.

JAY: What the hell does that mean?

AMANDA: Look, we can't really plan anything until after Reykjavik. Let's talk then.

JAY: We both know the truth. I can't make Reykjavik happen unless I know your staying is still a possibility.

AMANDA: Jay, you already agreed to this.

JAY: Now I'm changing my mind. Is there or is there not a possibility of you staying?

AMANDA: Everything's fine for right now.

JAY: Damn straight it's fine. You have no idea how hard I'll fight to keep you. Block every loan. Poison every client.

AMANDA: You son of a bitch.

JAY: Don't act surprised. You know my ways. The same things are in you.

(AMANDA *shakes her head "no".)*

JAY: It's okay. There's no judgment between us. There can't be.

AMANDA: Nothing else bad can happen. Not even a hint of a whisper.

JAY: If—

AMANDA: I mean it this time.

(JAY *takes* AMANDA*'s hands. Before he can speak…)*

AMANDA: No more words. Action. Otherwise, I swear I'll—

(JAY *wraps* AMANDA *in an embrace.)*

(End Scene)

Scene 5

(GOLDIE *works at her desk. She is now sort of chic.* REAGAN *enters.)*

REAGAN: Here's our overachiever.

(REAGAN *hands* GOLDIE *a document.)*

REAGAN: The executed copy of your NDA.

GOLDIE: I would've come to get it.

REAGAN: I needed to stretch my legs. I love running my little fiefdom, but it's good to come here and breathe in real power once in a while. *(She sits, puts her feet in the sand box.)*

GOLDIE: Is that what it's for?

REAGAN: Jay has the sand changed every week.

GOLDIE: Do you swim?

REAGAN: No. It's weird to be taking your clothes off at work.

GOLDIE: I know, right?

REAGAN: Congrats by the way. Your app predicting that sales drop saved us. Nice hit for your first week. Everybody's eyes were on Iceland. We might have missed it.

GOLDIE: You know how hard we have to work.

REAGAN: We?

GOLDIE: We're the only two women of color I've seen above the twenty fifth floor.

REAGAN: And?

GOLDIE: That makes us natural allies.

REAGAN: Just like that?

GOLDIE: Is that offensive?

REAGAN: I'm not offended. I just don't see myself as a woman of color. I'm black.

GOLDIE: Oh my goodness. You're a Republican. I shouldn't have assumed.

REAGAN: For someone who writes great code, you don't have such a good grip on statistics. I don't care how many times they trot out Diamond and Silk. Black women republicans are like unicorns. Rarely seen in the wild.

GOLDIE: I've put my foot in it again.

REAGAN: Forget it. I don't care about the Dems or Republicans. I'm independent. Want my vote? Work for it.

GOLDIE: That makes a lot of sense.

REAGAN: Can you vote? Your immigration status. The rules are so complicated.

GOLDIE: And always changing. Not yet. But I can't wait.

REAGAN: No need to rush. It seems like the things most of us want, never get voted in. I used to bust my butt volunteering for campaigns.

GOLDIE: But now?

REAGAN: Can't keep doing the same thing and expecting different results. It's all about community service for me now.

GOLDIE: I feel like I've got so much to learn from you. Would you consider being a kind of mentor?

REAGAN: What would I get out of it?

GOLDIE: I'm sorry?

REAGAN: Corporate America is all about an exchange. What would I get out of the deal?

GOLDIE: I guess I'll have to think about that one.

REAGAN: Thinking's good. I wish all my clients would embrace it.

GOLDIE: Your clients? Isn't that us?

REAGAN: Jay can be…I guess genius is close to madness. I wind up doing as much work for him as I do for the whole company?

GOLDIE: What do you mean?

REAGAN: Attorney client privilege. I guess if he rolled any other way, he wouldn't be Jay.

GOLDIE: That wouldn't be good.

REAGAN: Exactly. No way I'm voluntarily getting off this gravy train. Wait till bonuses come around. We make crazy money.

GOLDIE: What happens if Amanda moves to London?

REAGAN: No idea. The way I understand it, she'd still be tied to JayVision but we haven't discussed it. Personally, I don't think we have anything to worry about.

GOLDIE: She seemed very passionate about it.

REAGAN: I can't make any guarantees, obviously. But this is Wall Street, it's always smart to have a back-up plan, or two.

GOLDIE: Do you have one?

(REAGAN *smiles like a Cheshire cat.* GOLDIE *smiles.*)

REAGAN: Discretion's why I went to law school. My face used to give it all away.

GOLDIE: If not mentor, ally?

REAGAN: That's to be determined.

GOLDIE: I'll make it my business to make it in your interest.

REAGAN: I like the way my mom used to describe work. "It's like everyone's in their own small boat, and the boats are tied together by the thinnest of ropes. You're all rowing in the same direction, but those threads can snap any time.

GOLDIE: I choose to be optimistic. JayVision's starting to feel like family to me.

REAGAN: People always say that like it's a good thing. Almost every family I know is dysfunctional as hell.

GOLDIE: Can you be more candid with me than that?

REAGAN: Not yet. When I get back from Reykjavik, we'll see.

GOLDIE: Success!

(End Scene)

Scene 6

(The office is not visible. We're in "Iceland" with its dramatic lighting on the stage monitors and projected around and through the audience. JAY and REAGAN run through the audience holding hands and laughing.)

(They reach the edge of the stage which is now the water's edge in Reykjavik. JAY wears a wet suit under an deer skin duster. REAGAN is bundled into a fur coat. They take in Reykjavik's spring time beauty.)

REAGAN: There's no high like closing a deal.

JAY: It's not the deal. It's me, definitely. Admit it.

REAGAN: Okay, you win, partially.

JAY: You are such a lawyer. Eight at night and it's like high noon. This is a long way from Fresno.

REAGAN: That really where you're from? Cause I've got cousins from there, you don't sound like—

JAY: What the hell, we're a million miles from home. I hail from Clovis. A two cow, railroad town. Don't ask me how a bunch of Jews wound up there.

REAGAN: The diaspora's powerful. It carves out places to thrive.

JAY: *(Laughs)* True that. Don't fucking tell anyone. You'll ruin the mystique.

REAGAN: It's even further away from Bed Stuy. Not in miles, but...

JAY: I know what you mean. I wish we had more time. I'd like to stay here and bask for awhile. Did you text Amanda?

REAGAN: I sent her some updates. I like to do my talking after the ink's dry.

JAY: Do they train esquires to find ways to shut down progress?

REAGAN: You're the sail. I'm the ballast. It's a productive tension.

(The Northern Lights emerge and blanket the stage and audience.)

REAGAN: Wow.

JAY: Surreal.

REAGAN: I finally get stark beauty. *(She takes out her cell phone.)*

JAY: Screw that. You can get better shots off Google. Live in the moment.

(REAGAN nods agreement.)

JAY: You done good, kid. It was Amanda's idea, but the deal? All you.

REAGAN: Did you notice I got the language in we wanted on exchange rates?

JAY: I tell everyone, hire black chicks.

Better educated, rock bottom prices. Except for you, my queen. I put you on a pedestal. Surrounded by a tsunami of money.

REAGAN: *(Laughs)* Every time I turn press the button in the Maybach, I think of you.

JAY: If you were at a firm, with the amount you owed in student loans? You'd be lucky to lease a Fiesta.

REAGAN: Creepy that you know that, but I give thanks.

JAY: Look, I've been funding civil rights for the last twenty years, way past when it was cool. Putting you into a Tesla proves my love is pure and my commitment, total. *(He lets his duster fall open. He pats the bulge.)*

REAGAN: Don't you see this kind of crap makes people think—

JAY: Think what? I'm no joke to the people I saved from the hurricane. Half the progressives in Congress are there because of me.

REAGAN: It looks bad.

JAY: Who gives a damn how anything looks? I win life on my terms. You are so whitey-fied.

REAGAN: Hey!

JAY: If I were in your shoes, the whole legal department would look like the NBA. I think you like being the only one.

REAGAN: Without Yale on my resumé, would you, the great liberal, have given me the time of day? I don't think so.

JAY: Finally, she starts to grow some balls.

REAGAN: I told you.

JAY: Sorry.

REAGAN: Don't talk to me like that. Step over the line with the rest of them, not me.

(JAY laughs.)

REAGAN: I mean it.

JAY: I said sorry. You're not the only black Ivy chick out here. You see them doing deals like this? JayVision's a little Wild West. News flash, the Wild West's the only path to opportunity for people like us.

REAGAN: I'm not saying you're one hundred percent wrong.

JAY: But you don't like it. Too bad. It's how things work.

REAGAN: I've conceded you were part right.

JAY: It's not a win until there's total concession.

REAGAN: Uncle.

(JAY *smiles, satisfied.*)

JAY: Say, how much does that charity of yours need? The Boys and Girls Club, right?

REAGAN: You're asking me that now?

JAY: There's never anything wrong with now.

REAGAN: Six-hundred-and-thirty-seven thousand dollars. I know it's a lot. But that includes a hundred thousand to start an endowment. We've put a lot of thought into it.

(Beat)

JAY: I'm not volunteering shit.

REAGAN: You brought it up.

JAY: You want it? You've gotta ask. Squeaky wheel gets the grease.

REAGAN: Could you, would you be willing to consider a…ten thousand dollar donation?

JAY: Those mofos are screwed if they're depending on you. They can't wipe their ass with ten K.

REAGAN: Those children aren't anybody's motherfuckers.

JAY: Now you sound black.

REAGAN: You can really be an a-hole.

(JAY *puts on his reading glasses and starts texting.*)

REAGAN: You're just going to ignore me now?

(JAY *finally stops texting.*)

JAY: Five hundred thousand in the next check run.

REAGAN: Jesus.

JAY: That's how the wild west rolls.

REAGAN: Are you sure? From the bottom of—

JAY: Don't gush. I hate that shit.

REAGAN: *(Warmly)* Fuck you.

JAY: There you go.

REAGAN: I'm blown away. You're literally the best boss I've ever had. I have no idea how to feel about that.

JAY: I recommend learning to live with ambivalence. It's served me well.

(REAGAN *starts leaving.*)

JAY: Where are you going?

REAGAN: To tell them. They're going to freak.

JAY: If you want, I can come with. We can call together.

(JAY *strokes* REAGAN's *arm. She freezes.*)

JAY: I wasn't trying—I didn't want to let the moment go.

REAGAN: I'll see you at the party tonight. *(She leaves.)*

JAY: Fuck! Fuck, fuck, fuck. *(He is enraged, then desolate. He calls* AMANDA.*)* Mandy, pick up. *(No answer.)* You're supposed to be at my disposal when I'm away. Who do these bitches think they are? Reagan walking off with my money without a look back? Under normal circumstances, I wouldn't even think about banging her. But I'm here at the top of my game. And Iceland's fucking amazing. This deal's the most legit thing I've ever done. I deserve some freaking gratification. *(He rubs his belly, then his thighs. He begins to pound his*

flesh, fighting desire.) It's always been this way. Me
against my needs. In college, when I played water
polo I always won the same way. I'd hold the other
man underwater. First they'd fight me with fierceness.
Slowly, they'd cross into submission. Then I'd let them
up gently, lovingly. By then, they couldn't get to the
surface without my help. After that I'd throw my arms
around them. Feel the trembling as their lungs filled
with air.
That's what I love, the tenderness after the breaking. It
makes me whole.

(End Scene)

Scene 7

*(GOLDIE works. The monitors broadcast images of JAY
winning [!] at business, sports, life, and events. The elevator
opens. KESHA and AMANDA enter in boy shorts and a
swimsuit respectively.)*

GOLDIE: Hey.

KESHA: You should've joined us. It's a JayVision
tradition once we've nailed a deal.

AMANDA: Jay's motto. Deny yourself nothing.

KESHA: Never wait to celebrate.

AMANDA: He had the nerve to call me last night
when he should have been working on our next
breakthrough.

GOLDIE: I can't wait to hear all the details.

AMANDA: The details are we're about to get paid.

KESHA: We should throw a pool party for the whole
company. Invite the lower floors.

AMANDA: Blasphemy! Besides, lady esquire's too good
for the pool. Worried about her hair.

GOLDIE: With some justification. From what I've heard—

AMANDA: Please. She's privileged as hell.

KESHA: I went to a public school that couldn't even qualify as shitty. One hundred percent free lunch while her highness sailed through boarding school.

AMANDA: Secretarial college wasn't exactly mind expanding. Andover then Yale and we still have to listen to the oppression Olympics.

KESHA: Be fair, you come from money.

AMANDA: We *had* money. But my father was a bastard. He broke us and left us with nothing but the trappings of money.

(KESHA *touches* AMANDA's *arm.*)

AMANDA: *(Beat. To* GOLDIE*)* You haven't said anything.

GOLDIE: This is all in good fun, right?

KESHA: Congratulations!

AMANDA: You've passed the PC test.

GOLDIE: There's nothing wrong with water cooler talk.

(AMANDA *and* KESHA *applaud.*)

GOLDIE: I thought you might be trying to goose me. Watch out, I am learning your ways.

AMANDA: We used to have a literal water cooler. JayVision's first digs were in a fifth floor walk up. In Long Island City before gentrification. The bathroom was in the basement. I lived in terror of having to march back upstairs in heels and hose. Back then, Jay was a leg man. Be glad you didn't have to live through that.

GOLDIE: *(Takes a chance)* Okay boomer!

AMANDA: Catch!

(AMANDA *spikes the volleyball to* GOLDIE, *who misses it.*
AMANDA *pumps her arms in triumph.* AMANDA *retrieves
the ball, then pats* GOLDIE'*s shoulder.*)

AMANDA: See? I can take a joke and I don't always
have to win.

KESHA: What did I tell you? Best boss ever.

(KESHA *and* AMANDA *stretch out on their towels.*)

KESHA: He let me be lead on my first deal. I hadn't
been here six months.

GOLDIE: Amazing.

KESHA: I was scared shitless. I must've worked
nineteen hour days for weeks. If we hadn't had
showers and a pool? (*She displays hairy armpits.*) You
see what's going on here. Even Birkenstock lesbos
would've called me out.

GOLDIE: Off of that.

(GOLDIE *retrieves sparkling waters for* AMANDA *and*
KESHA.)

AMANDA: You cannot be this good. Because if you are,
then my whole life's a lie.

GOLDIE: It's a small gesture.

KESHA: No one wants to work with people who act like
they're better than everybody else.

GOLDIE: I'm so not!

AMANDA: Then we demand salacious details from your
past.

GOLDIE: I'm kind of a private person.

(KESHA *lobs the volley ball at* GOLDIE. GOLDIE *retrieves it.
When she turns around,* KESHA *grabs her and covers her
eyes.* AMANDA *takes* GOLDIE'*s hands and marches her into
the sandbox.*)

GOLDIE: Guys!

AMANDA: This is sand.

GOLDIE: It's not funny.

KESHA: Hazing's serious business. Still it's got to be done.

(AMANDA *throws a cup of ice onto* GOLDIE'*s feet.*)

AMANDA: Sand, then ice. Ice, then fire.

GOLDIE: Stop! It hurts.

AMANDA: *(To* KESHA*)* Okay, that's enough.

KESHA: Is it?

(KESHA *releases* KESHA, *grabs a lighter and flicks it on.*)

KESHA: We demand red meat for our hungry maws.

(AMANDA *takes away the lighter.*)

AMANDA: That's too much. You okay?

GOLDIE: I'm fine, but I told you. I'm a private person.

AMANDA: Do you know how many hoops we jumped through for your visa? Shouldn't you share?

KESHA: We won't relent until we drag you down to our level.

AMANDA: Sorry, that's just the way it is.

GOLDIE: Okay, okay.

(KESHA *rubs her hands together in anticipation.*)

GOLDIE: If you must know, I had sex with my high school principal.

AMANDA: Girl or guy?

GOLDIE: Guy.

KESHA: I knew you were a secret freak.

GOLDIE: Not the kind of sex that would disqualify me from being a virgin. It was all very secret and very wrong.

KESHA: Details.

GOLDIE: Never.

AMANDA: Are you ashamed?

GOLDIE: It was bomb.

(They all laugh.)

GOLDIE: If you ever tell—

KESHA: Who'd believe us?

AMANDA: With this revelation, you are officially invited to the office hang tonight. O'Doul's, seven-thirty PM.

GOLDIE: I don't drink.

AMANDA: We don't care. Fun's mandatory.

KESHA: *(German accent)* You vill be there and you vill—

(AMANDA's phone rings.)

AMANDA: Stirling here. When? What?
Got it. *(To KESHA)* Get dressed.

GOLDIE: What happened?

AMANDA: A little deal hiccup.

(KESHA rushes out.)

GOLDIE: Can I help?

AMANDA: We'll see. I need the office. Now. Take a long lunch. Go!

(GOLDIE hustles out. AMANDA dials her phone.)

AMANDA: Intercontinental Hotel VIP, please. Amanda Stirling, executive associate of JayVision here. I understand there's allegations about the yacht? Slow down. Slow. Down. Stop. What's your name? *(She takes notes on a pad.)* Jessica? Jessica, stop repeating what you think the hotel's policy is. Policies aren't law. I need you to focus. I'm on the phone with you. We're going to resolve this issue together. But let's talk to each other like human beings. *(Listens)* Is this alleged victim okay? Good. That's the most important thing. Write that down. You're not trying to collect for the sheets, but the massage table and drapes have to be paid for. Understood and done. You see? We're making progress. *(Listens)* Why do you have to contact your supervisor? What's his name? *(She looks up Jim's information on her laptop.)* Jim's not there. You're in charge. Show some initiative. We spend thousands of dollars a year with you. I'm sure Jim— *(The ploy doesn't work.)* Okay, I understand. But I strongly suggest you not contact the police without unimpeachable evidence that Mr Littleton is guilty of something. I'll wait for your call.

(KESHA *enters.* AMANDA *holds up a finger.)*

AMANDA: And don't worry about any costs. We'll take care of those regardless. Good will between long term partners. *(She hangs up.)*

KESHA: What do you need?

AMANDA: Get this Jim guy on the phone. Explain our position. Find out what he needs. What did you find out? I need good news.

KESHA: The *Post* won't run anything.

AMANDA: Good. Page Six is a scourge.

KESHA: The other outlets are still pending.

AMANDA: Find out what they want and give it to them. Don't start with money. We have to do the little dance. Then reach out to our contacts at Bloomberg. Take them to lunch, an expensive lunch. Take the *Journal* gal to dinner.

KESHA: Lesbian cabal?

AMANDA: Take one for the team if you have to.

KESHA: She's hot. Consider it done.

AMANDA: Tomorrow work TMZ. Offer them the normal kill fee.

KESHA: If they get greedy?

AMANDA: Promise them the next exclusive.

KESHA: PR's taken care of. Our donation to HAF will be on CBS This Morning.

AMANDA: I knew there was a reason I liked you.

KESHA: Are you okay?

AMANDA: Just pissed. A little scared. We closed it. What the hell happened?

KESHA: I can stay.

AMANDA: I need you more out there.

KESHA: We've been here before. We've got this.

(KESHA *impulsively kisses* AMANDA *on the cheek, then leaves.*)

(AMANDA video calls JAY. She is annoyed. The monitors show JAY's hotel suite. There's a broken massage table and blood spattered drapes. We can't see Jay.

JAY: *(OS)* Mandy?

AMANDA: What are you still doing on the yacht?

JAY: Is it safe for me to leave?

AMANDA: The hell is wrong with you? Move the camera!

(JAY *sobs.*)

AMANDA: You're creating a record. Documentation. Nod if you understand.

(JAY *shakily moves the camera frame to a pristine area.*)

AMANDA: Do I have to…? Show yourself.

(JAY *appears. He looks like a chastened school boy.*)

JAY: (*Whispers*) I screwed—

AMANDA: Not over an open line. It's being taken care of.

JAY: (*Aggressively*) Look, I swear to you—

AMANDA: What do you swear on this time? Your mother? Your children?

JAY: I need you to listen. If you'd just listen for once.

AMANDA: Not over an open line. (*She shuts off the call.*)

(*The monitors turn on. We see three* WOMEN'*s hands violently scrubbing a blood streaked mattress cover. We don't see their faces.*)

WOMAN 3: It's happening again.

AMANDA: Shut up. Shut up—

WOMAN 2: You're tied at the hip. Didn't you have a feeling? A hint?

AMANDA: None.

WOMAN 3: So you had no idea?

AMANDA: I'm here. Doing my goddamned job. He's thousands of miles away. How in the hell am I supposed to—?

WOMAN 2: The question. Is past prologue?

WOMAN 1: Can the future be rewritten?

WOMAN 3: Or is it too hard to leave the warmth of the sun?

(*The monitors emit* JAY'*s beam of light.*)

WOMAN 3: So inviting. So blinding.

(AMANDA *rushes to turn the monitors off. When she does, we still hear their voices.*)

(*The* WOMEN *sigh.*)

WOMAN 1: *(OS)* Clean up time.

WOMAN 3: *(OS)* Time to set the machine in motion.

WOMAN 2: *(OS)* Again. How does it feel?

AMANDA: You've no right to judge me.

(*The monitors go dark.*)

WOMAN 2: *(OS)* Oops. Don't look too closely.

AMANDA: I don't have any facts before me. Neither do you.

WOMAN 2: *(OS)* But you're not quite sure.

WOMAN 3: *(OS)* Signs are imperfect communications.

AMANDA: I don't put myself in such situations so I wouldn't know.

WOMAN 2: *(OS)* But you've been there. Perhaps on both sides?

AMANDA: There's such a thing as blurred lines.

WOMAN 1: *(OS)* Perfect assaults go unpunished, too.

AMANDA: What do you mean by perfect?

WOMAN 3: *(OS)* Defensive wounds, tears, abrasions.

WOMAN 2: *(OS)* Screams.

AMANDA: An impossible standard. The yacht is soundproof.

WOMEN: Mmmmm.

AMANDA: Who even says there was an assault?

WOMAN 1: *(OS)* There's blood.

AMANDA: Who initiated the letting?

WOMAN 3: *(OS)* In life, we move on a sixty to seventy per cent certainty.

WOMAN 2: *(OS)* With rape, the discussion doesn't start unless things hit ninety six per cent.

WOMEN: *(OS)* Maybe.

AMANDA: I want to believe them every single time. The stories always fall apart like wet paper bags. And the story always ends the same way. They come for the money.

WOMAN 1: If it was available, we're sure they'd ask for time travel.

WOMAN 3: Where's the quantum realm when you really need it?

AMANDA: If they don't want cash, they demand a hook up. How am I supposed to respect that?

WOMAN 2: *(OS. Whispers)* Would things fall apart without your expertise?

AMANDA: You don't get to impugn my motives. I've mentored dozens of women.

WOMAN 2: *(OS)* You've also fed the machine.

AMANDA: Get out!

WOMAN 2: *(OS)* Once we leave, what's left?

WOMAN 1: *(OS)* Lotty. London. Crossroads.

(End Scene)

END OF ACT ONE

ACT TWO

Scene 1

(Early morning. GOLDIE *works fitfully.* KESHA *enters.)*

KESHA: You're here early.

GOLDIE: To find out what the heck's going on. What kind of trouble are we in?

KESHA: Jay's stuck in Iceland a little longer. Bureaucratic snag.

GOLDIE: There's got to be more to it than that. The building's buzzing.

KESHA: Something about Jay and a woman. The usual. Nothing to worry about.

GOLDIE: My parents blew up my phone yesterday. They're completely freaked out.

KESHA: Even I don't have the full picture. I don't feel comfortable serving you up the drips and drabs I think I know. Reagan'll lay everything out for us.

GOLDIE: Why not Amanda?

KESHA: If this thing turns legal everything needs be scrutinized very carefully.

GOLDIE: If?

KESHA: Stop trying to worm something out of me. Amanda doesn't appreciate cross talk.

GOLDIE: Amanda doesn't need a visa to stay here.

KESHA: Our kitten does have claws.

GOLDIE: If Iceland doesn't happen, we're still good, right?

KESHA: Profits are solid.

GOLDIE: What about our reputation? Future prospects? I can construct a predictive model.

KESHA: There's nothing to worry about. We've survived worse. We always win.

GOLDIE: Kesha, it's not just me I'm worried about. My parents are counting on me to sponsor them.

KESHA: I hadn't thought of that.

GOLDIE: You know how it is. I'm sure you help your folks.

KESHA: Why would I do that? I came out. They kicked me to the curb. End of story.

GOLDIE: That's awful.

KESHA: I'm over it. Get work done. That's what counts. This'll blow over.

GOLDIE: You're sure?

KESHA: We've beaten back every disturbance to the zone. But when things get back to normal, Jay and Amanda will have forgotten about all this distraction. You'll be judged on your production. Focus on that.

GOLDIE: How many times have you been through this?

KESHA: I already told you, we don't know what "this" is.

GOLDIE: I thought I was a full member of the team?

KESHA: At the moment, no one's asking for your participation. Count yourself lucky.

GOLDIE: What do I say if my parents call me on it again?

KESHA: You come from one of those perky sitcom families, don't you? Finally, I've got a kid sister I can corrupt.

GOLDIE: *(Laughs)* Or take under your wing. Amanda's obviously grooming you to take her spot.

KESHA: Reagan turn you down?

GOLDIE: *(Busted)* Yup.

KESHA: *(Laughs)* She's like that.

GOLDIE: She called you Amanda's heir apparent.

KESHA: I don't know if I want her job. Jay's never going to forgive whoever steps into that spot for not being her. Who knows? Maybe I'll try London.

GOLDIE: Really?

KESHA: Jay put me on. I'll be eternally grateful for that. But I really feel like Amanda and I could build something.

GOLDIE: If you and Amanda bail—

KESHA: It wouldn't be bailing. No one owes, Goldie.

GOLDIE: Okay. Then do you have any advice to spare?

KESHA: JayVision's like the hardware store I worked at every summer, Powell's. Powell's wife was the sweetest thing. She knew her way around hardware better than any guy I've seen. They were printing money. Even the new Home Depot didn't break them.

GOLDIE: Not many places can stand up to those big box stores. They must've had a ton of good will.

KESHA: Screw good will. They knew what they were doing. You ask me, that's half of Jay's zone. He doesn't fall for the bullshit. He doesn't look at resumes. All he wants to know is, do the people in place know what the fuck they're doing? Making money, yea or nay?

GOLDIE: That's succinct.

KESHA: Anyway, the wife'd tell you what to buy and what to do. You'd pay him. He'd bellow, snatch the cash and send you on your way. Anyway, when my parents fell off senior year, Powell paid my whole tuition, cash. Not a word spoken. Jay's just another Powell.

GOLDIE: What about Amanda?

KESHA: You don't get it. There's no difference between Jay and Amanda. Let her help you. Let him bellow. Just make sure you never let them cross your line. Do that and you're fucked.

GOLDIE: Sounds like a *Survivor* episode.

KESHA: America's a *Survivor* episode.

GOLDIE: It shouldn't have to be. There's literally so much here.

KESHA: Doesn't bother me. My family's straight trailer trash. JayVision's an improvement. I'm used to men with boulders carved onto their shoulders. Loud and wrong.

GOLDIE: You're doing great now. Maybe everything worked out the way it was supposed to.

KESHA: Jay and Amanda can be loud and wrong. Look at this Iceland mess. Watch yourself.

(AMANDA *enters.* KESHA *and* GOLDIE *freeze. Did she hear?*)

AMANDA: *(To* KESHA*)* I need you.

KESHA: Coming.

AMANDA: I didn't hear what you said. But now I know you two are in cahoots. *(To* GOLDIE*)* Boo!

(GOLDIE *jumps.*)

AMANDA: As long as you follow her lead, you'll be fine. Right, Kesha?

KESHA: Roger that boss.

AMANDA: Mmmmm.

(AMANDA *and* KESHA *exit.*)

(*End Scene*)

Scene 2

(*Empty office. Dawn on Sunday. Screens flicker on showing* JAY, *sitting in a deck chair on the rooftop pool. He surveils his kingdom in close ups and full shots.*)

(*He sits splay-legged in a Speedo and cover up, but seems naked despite them. The door opens. The screens dim.*)

(AMANDA *blows a kiss to her daughter as the elevator door closes.*)

AMANDA: (*Into her phone*) You've seen me safely to my destination. Bye darling.

(*A camera sound.*)

AMANDA: I know you're there.

(JAY *enters from the elevator. He hangs his head sheepishly.*)

JAY: Busted. (*He sits legs splayed.*) It smells like young girl. You should have let Lotty come in. It's been so long since—

AMANDA: You're supposed to be on house arrest in your apartment.

JAY: House. Arrest. Such jarring terms.

AMANDA: Follow the plan.

JAY: I'm not feeling the love.

AMANDA: Close them.

(JAY *doesn't move.* AMANDA *parts her legs.*)

JAY: Is this consensual?

AMANDA: It was the quickest way to get you to focus. (*She crosses her legs.*)

AMANDA: I mean it.

(JAY *doesn't close his legs, but zooms the camera out.*)

JAY: Do you ever stop to think that as an older man I have certain vulnerabilities?

AMANDA: Shit.

(AMANDA *and* JAY *laugh.*)

JAY: What are you freaking out about? I've never been under indictment. No warrants, convictions. Not even a traffic ticket.

AMANDA: You've been lucky.

JAY: What I am is innocent.

AMANDA: This claim looks bogus. I agree.

JAY: Fraudulent, fabricated, fucked up—

AMANDA: Yes to all that. I get it. People with ovaries lie, too. But if we don't get this completely cleaned up, you'll have an international conviction. That threatens everything.

JAY: London?

AMANDA: Everything. And yes, that includes London.

JAY: I'm racing as fast as I can to keep my promises to you and everybody else.

AMANDA: You're also busy tearing everything down at the same time.

JAY: When is somebody going to give a damn about the toll all this is taking on me? Everyone's clawing at me. Where is it? When do I get mine? Who's here for me?

AMANDA: Me, a team of investigators, lawyers, crisis management. Your wife and kids.

JAY: They're my dependents. They've got to play along.

AMANDA: As long as you haven't lost your sense of humor, we're still in it.

JAY: Who do these Iceland a-holes think they are? Eight days in their country, showering them with my money and they want to brand me as a sex offender? I need a wartime consigliere. Are you up for it?

AMANDA: Is your generation of men ever going to let *The Godfather* go?

JAY: Some men would punch you in the face for saying that.

AMANDA: If they do, I'll give as good as I get.

JAY: This is why you'll always be my number one. We're Jordan and Pippen. Batman and Robin. Dom and slave.

AMANDA: Robin got his own comic book and Pippen went out on his own.

JAY: Who remembers Pippen from Houston? Like it or not, this is your legacy, baby. Everyone else? To this day, Ethel and Jay Sr have never fully supported me.

AMANDA: Stop it. Your parents are lovely.

JAY: To you. Their commitment to loveliness didn't start till they started getting paid. If anything goes wrong, I'm suing Iceland oblivion.

AMANDA: We need to tread carefully. We don't have a framework in place to handle international.

JAY: Why the fuck not?

AMANDA: We didn't fucking think we'd need it.

JAY: I pay you to anticipate challenges.

AMANDA: You agreed to stop creating them.

JAY: I asked. Directly. She giggled, never gave me a straight answer. As far I could tell, it was all systems go.

AMANDA: You've put us in the hands of a vengeful child.

JAY: Iceland's age of consent is fifteen.

AMANDA: The finance minister's daughter. What were you thinking?

JAY: What was she doing at an adult party? Where's her mother's responsibility?

AMANDA: The girl never identified herself? Was she officially announced?

(JAY *shakes his head "no".*)

AMANDA: Great. Are you absolutely sure?

JAY: We were high off the deal. You know what that's like. Reagan and I were freaking killing it.

AMANDA: Reagan—

JAY: Oh, get over yourself with Reagan.

AMANDA: I'll get this to the team. This might be what we need to put this whole thing to bed.

JAY: Friends again?

AMANDA: Not yet.

JAY: I wasn't the only older man she came on to. The girl's mother shouldn't have let her come to an adult party dressed like that. I swear to god, Mandy. She looked like she was twenty-five.

AMANDA: Who else? We can use that.

JAY: Whatever sad one hit wonder they had singing. He took off right away, probably to sing that pitiful dirge somewhere else.

AMANDA: Anyone else?

JAY: That toadie from the EU. He blew her off.

(AMANDA *glares.*)

JAY: Right. Wise in retrospect. But in the heat of the moment.

AMANDA: Reagan didn't mention this. Can she confirm any of it?

JAY: She was chatting up the bankers. You know how it is. They all went to school together.

AMANDA: This is still more than we had to work with.

JAY: She shouldn't be allowed to get away with it.

AMANDA: Do you want me to say there's no double standard? We both know there is.

JAY: She's changed her story. Is she even stable? Should we offer her counseling?

AMANDA: No way. It would look like an admission of guilt after...

JAY: After Allison.

AMANDA: Let's not relitigate the past.

JAY: Everyone promises things calm down with age. I call bullshit. Everything in me's stronger: insights, urges.

AMANDA: Figure it out.

JAY: It is in you, too. I can feel it. What if she shows up here? You know how things are now. I'd be the violator.

AMANDA: Which is why you were asked to lie low. You set the table. They decide what's on the menu.

JAY: You've never made a big deal like this. Nobody's got a sense of humor anymore.

AMANDA: Maybe I've been doing you a disservice covering for you.

JAY: Covering for me? What does that even mean? We're a team, darlin'.

AMANDA: I keep having to remind you. It's been a really long while.

JAY: I know what lurks in your heart.

AMANDA: Look at how much coin's going to private eyes, publicists, operatives. God only know how much Iceland's going to cost us.

JAY: We're swimming in cash.

AMANDA: Money doesn't cover everything. *(She puts her head in her hands.)*

JAY: Tired?

AMANDA: Spent.

JAY: We gone into battle in worse shape.

AMANDA: This has to be the last time.

JAY: I know my word's not good enough any more. I'm taking responsibility. I've got a lead on some international investigators. Bulgarians. These guys are smooth.

AMANDA: We can't manage this girl. She's got an entire government behind her. Reagan and I will handle this.

JAY: Smooth things over with her? I feel terrible about her getting detained.

AMANDA: Did you even try to help her?

JAY: When I saw the FBI I freaked. They sent five guys built like pro wrestlers. Like I'm some kind of terrorist. God, I need you.

AMANDA: Come.

(JAY opens his arms. AMANDA accepts the hug.)

JAY: I'll make it up to you.

(AMANDA nods.)

JAY: We've got to keep Reagan on board.

AMANDA: If she wanted to jump ship, she would've done it already.

JAY: We need her enthusiastic participation. She's still angry. Defang her, but leave her fired up enough to fight. It's a delicate balance.

AMANDA: She never shuts up about equity. Let's give her some.

JAY: What are you thinking?

AMANDA: Fifty/fifty. Fifty percent women straight up and down the chain: vendors, board, executives, special emphasis on BIPOCs.

JAY: She's not stupid. JayVision's already there. Women run this place.

AMANDA: Not really. But what if we push for fifty/fifty across the industry? That'll make a splash. And fresh ink means…

JAY: Eyes off Iceland. Brilliant. I knew you had it.

AMANDA: We reset as the industry leader, with the first pick at talent.

JAY: You're setting the table for London.

AMANDA: You asked me to turn shit into opportunity. Why shouldn't I get to enjoy some of the spoils?

JAY: Of course you should. I wouldn't respect you if you didn't, but I'll still try to get you to stay.

AMANDA: You can try.

JAY: I'm going to take you to Iceland to see the lights one day. You'd be so inspired. I think you might even start painting again. You haven't touched a brush in so long.

AMANDA: Go.

(JAY *leaves.*)

WOMAN 1: *(OS)* A reckoning?

WOMAN 2: A turning away? Or an embrace?

(AMANDA dials.)

AMANDA: Reagan?

(End Scene)

Scene 3

(After hours. AMANDA lays in wait. REAGAN enters, kicks off her shoes, and soothes her feet in the sand box.)

AMANDA: What took so long?

REAGAN: Do you read your texts? International's a whole different beast. I was lucky to make it back here this soon. But we're set.

AMANDA: Good job.

REAGAN: We'll see. I'm calling a car. You want one?

AMANDA: No. Why didn't you at least try to stop him?

REAGAN: Don't you dare try to put this on me.

AMANDA: You knew what could happen.

REAGAN: Legally, I do not. And so what if I did? Jay had hours to say, "hey, something went down wrong. The FBI might be waiting for us at JFK". He said not one word.

AMANDA: He assured me he didn't know.

REAGAN: They held me for two hours. My bar card didn't make much of an impression.

AMANDA: That shouldn't have happened. I'll make some calls.

REAGAN: Oh please. What, are you going to call Iceland's manager? I'm never going through humiliation like that again for the company.

AMANDA: Is that a threat?

REAGAN: Not against you.

AMANDA: Would it have killed you to have a few drinks?

REAGAN: Go for a couples massage? That didn't work out so well for Allison. And she just watched. Allegedly.

AMANDA: If Jay's this monster, why did she just thank him—profusely—in the *Journal*?

REAGAN: It's beyond me.

AMANDA: You know that all any woman has to do is tell him 'no.' No mixed signals, a New York 'no' and it stops. Be honest. You've had to do it, I'm sure.

REAGAN: I've drawn a line. He respects it.

AMANDA: Then so could anybody else. That leaves us with questions. Why didn't that happen here? What was all the flirting about?

REAGAN: There was a lot of blood.

AMANDA: There's been blood before. Along with consent, and no convictions. He likes it rough. Everybody likes it that way sometimes.

REAGAN: I told you from the beginning. I'm not a fixer.

AMANDA: You just hire and direct them. Make sure their paperwork is within the legal lines.

REAGAN: Maybe we should've had this out before. I don't know what your deal is with Jay. Muse, partner, shrink, whipping girl.

AMANDA: All of the above. Proudly.

REAGAN: Good for you. JayVision's not paying me enough to risk my license. You want London? I've got ambitions of my own.

AMANDA: Oh?

REAGAN: I need this deal to close as much you do. So trust me I'll do my part.

AMANDA: What do you have going on?

(REAGAN *doesn't answer.*)

AMANDA: Keep your secrets.

REAGAN: I intend to.

(AMANDA *sits beside* REAGAN, *and puts her feet in the sandbox.*)

AMANDA: Let's have a Mr Rogers' moment so we can strategize clearly. We say things we don't mean when we're emotional.

REAGAN: What's the ask?

AMANDA: How far can our investigators go in Iceland?

REAGAN: They've got much stronger privacy laws.

AMANDA: Get us right up to the line. We need all the grays.

REAGAN: Will do. (*She struggles into her shoes.*)

AMANDA: I never thought we'd find ourselves in this spot again. I truly thought Allison was the end of it.

REAGAN: Sure.

AMANDA: Are you sure this one's winnable?

REAGAN: The government still needs this to happen, but won't go hard against the mom, at least not publicly. I'd say eighty, twenty.

AMANDA: She's probably angry and embarrassed.

REAGAN: Wouldn't you be?

AMANDA: It's our job to get her past it.

REAGAN: That's your job.

AMANDA: It's everyone's job.

REAGAN: For now.

AMANDA: If the Finance Minister has any vulnerabilities, that would help our negotiating position enormously.

REAGAN: Why would we look into her? Even discussing it's unbelievably risky.

AMANDA: If there are vulnerabilities, we need to exploit them. I'm not talking about things that would traumatize the girl. Just things that would cause her to reflect on the greater good.

REAGAN: I won't get you ammunition if that's what you're asking.

AMANDA: Develop the evidence.

REAGAN: Sure.

AMANDA: My daughter's only a few years younger than this woman. Whatever went down, I feel for her. When you become a mom, your heart grows so big, it starts living outside your body. Haven't I ever mommed you?

REAGAN: You must be thinking of Kesha.

AMANDA: Why can't we be easy with each other?

REAGAN: The girl's name is Helmi. I'll see what I can do.

AMANDA: I'm counting on you.

REAGAN: This is about London. Isn't it?

AMANDA: This is my last shot. It's been six years in the making. I haven't got another six in me.

(KESHA *enters.*)

AMANDA: Come on in. We're family. All our squabbles belong out in the open.

KESHA: Bonding moments would do wonders for you two. That or some great sex.

REAGAN: *(To* AMANDA*)* You promised you wouldn't tell.

KESHA: Thank goodness Goldie isn't here to witness this. You'd scare her half to death.

AMANDA: I need to roll calls. *(She exits.)*

KESHA: How're you holding up?

REAGAN: Truth?

KESHA: Nothing better.

REAGAN: I do not want to be dealing with this. I keep thinking about the Dr King quote. Am I killing myself to integrate into a burning house?

KESHA: Is there any other kind of house these days? Everything's on fire. The best we can hope for is to find somewhere to wait out the rain.

REAGAN: It feels like every time I get close to a real win, the bottom drops out. And not just me. Black people in general. I'm constantly recalibrating.

KESHA: Tell me about it. The hustle's real.

REAGAN: Don't tell me the teacher's pet is disgruntled?

KESHA: I know Iceland's going to work out, but it makes me sad.

REAGAN: I certainly don't need another trip to the Saving Jay From Himself gift shop. I've got all the mugs I need.

KESHA: All this is starting to remind me of home. I busted my ass to get away from there. And here I am looking at the same thing. Eruptions always threatening to boil over. Never enough to kill you and take you out of your misery. Just enough to scald. You know what, we should collude.

REAGAN: To what end?

KESHA: Tell me what you know. I'll give you my info.
If we get the whole picture for once, maybe we can cop
a piece of the action.

REAGAN: Nope. It's not right. I have a code of ethics.

KESHA: Tell me what would right would really look
like in this situation?

REAGAN: I converted to ethical relativism a long time
ago. Keeps me sane. Recommend.

KESHA: I always thought you were more righteous than
that.

REAGAN: I tried. For a long time, I tried. But I was poor
and you can't make moves without money.

(End Scene)

Scene 4

(GOLDIE and KESHA work.)

KESHA: Could you get me a latte from the indie place?

GOLDIE: Their line is atrocious.

KESHA: I know, but with the hours I've been pulling. I
need good quality caffeine.

GOLDIE: Got it.

KESHA: Not too much foam this time!

(GOLDIE exits. KESHA waits, then quickly dials the phone.)

KESHA: Hi! This is Kesha from JayVision calling about
your deposition. It's no big deal, five minutes max. I'm
calling to help you remember what happened. Thanks.
You say you saw Helmi on March 8th, but could you
be mistaken about the day? I'll put down that you're
unsure. Is that all right? You can call me back anytime

if you think of something. We'll compensate you for your time.

(KESHA *hangs up.* JAY *flickers on screen.*)

JAY: *(Laughs)* You're doing amazing, sweetie.

KESHA: You scared me.

JAY: I didn't mean to. Say, have we had you out to the house?

AMANDA: Not yet.

JAY: Why hasn't that happened? Montauk is a place of shocking beauty. You deserve that.

KESHA: I always promise myself I'm going to get out to Long Island, but it always falls through. You know, work.

JAY: If one wants a Brooklyn brownstone to play in, sacrifices have to be made. Besides, you love working hard.

KESHA: I do. Jay, what really happened in Iceland? You and the girl are the only ones who really know.

JAY: Would it change how you feel about me?

KESHA: No, I guess not really. I know you're not a bad man. But I still don't feel good about this.

JAY: You thinking of going to the media?

KESHA: Of course not. How could you even think that?

JAY: This thing has me paranoid. There's nothing to tell. It's all a misunderstanding.

KESHA: That's what I thought, but I keep thinking about Allison.

(JAY *reads* KESHA *carefully.*)

JAY: That was different. I fucked that up.

KESHA: You admit it?

JAY: Why wouldn't I? Haven't I always told you the truth, even when it's ugly?

KESHA: I've wanted to ask you for a long time. I don't know what I was so afraid of.

JAY: You should've.

KESHA: Amanda kinda of shut me down.

JAY: She can be bad that way. Fierce mama bear one minute, sorority sister the next. But how many women have got the range?

KESHA: And still hot.

JAY: You noticed.

KESHA: Yeah. You never pushed Allison into anything?

JAY: You mustn't tell anyone this, but she came on to me.

KESHA: I could sort of tell. Was it right after the Swindoll deal?

(JAY *nods.*)

KESHA: I thought so. She started swanning around like she owned the place. Straight women have got no game whatsoever.

JAY: Don't blame her. It was one hundred percent on me. I took advantage. *(Tears up)* I'm lucky you guys stuck with me. I've tried everything I can to make up for it. If there's something else you think I should do, especially for the LGBT...

KESHA: I'll let you know. Thanks.

JAY: I always want you feeling good.

KESHA: But—

(The doorbell sounds.)

JAY: My timing remains impeccable.

KESHA: What the hell?

JAY: Food delivery for you. Vegan extravaganza from Chloe.

KESHA: Fucking A. You remember that I went vegan?

JAY: I care about everyone and everything in this office.

(KESHA *grabs the food and rips it from its packaging.*)

JAY: Attack!

KESHA: Hey, I'm a bridge and tunnel gal. I've got no shame.

JAY: It's nice to see a woman enjoy her food. Most of the ones I know take twenty minutes to nibble a lettuce leaf to death.

KESHA: Screw that.

JAY: Enjoy. Tell me if there's anything wrong, okay?

KESHA: I make more money in a month than my parents made in a year. What problems could I have?

JAY: Then let's put Reykjavik out of its misery. It's time to move on.

(JAY *logs off.*)

WOMEN: *(OS. Whispers)* And with that...

(KESHA *is startled.* GOLDIE *enters.*)

GOLDIE: What's all this?

KESHA: Hand over the latte and dig in. Gift from Jay.

GOLDIE: This smells delicious. What else did I miss?

KESHA: Not a thing.

(End Scene)

Scene 5

(Early morning. GOLDIE *struggles in with a huge, clearly homemade packed box. She video calls* VIK.*)*

GOLDIE: Dad.

VIK: Morning.

GOLDIE: You cannot constantly be sending things to the office. It's not professional. It reeks of Indian food. They're not used to that here.

VIK: All right. I'm just happy my daughter takes time from slaying Wall Street dragons to talk with her father. And I worry about her. We hear things.

GOLDIE: I haven't slayed many yet. And there's no need to work. Things are calming down.

VIK: Bring up the sponsorship as soon as you can. A letter from the firm could make a huge difference.

GOLDIE: I will, but the timing's not right.

VIK: We trust your judgment. But, you know our situation. I heard about that girl making accusations. Disgusting to chase after a married man. Learn from this. Be very careful about being alone with any man.

GOLDIE: Oh I am, papa.

VIK: Don't let this business distract you. You're there for a purpose.

*(*REAGAN *enters.* GOLDIE *waves.)*

GOLDIE: They're taking good care of me.

VIK: Keep your head down. So, when are you coming home?

GOLDIE: It's a four hour ride.

VIK: Mother will pick you up from the train station.

GOLDIE: Fine. *(She clicks off.)*

GOLDIE: Sorry.

REAGAN: I understand, but you can't talk about anything that's going on with him. You could be deposed.

GOLDIE: He read about it. All he said was that a single woman shouldn't be alone with a man. I didn't and won't say anything.

REAGAN: That kind of talk keeps women from advancing. I'm alone with Jay all the time. Nothing's ever happened.

GOLDIE: That's good to know.

REAGAN: Everything's in how you handle yourself. If you try to play with a man, you're asking for it.

GOLDIE: This is all new to me. I've never been anywhere close to any sort of legal thing.

REAGAN: Welcome to Wall Street. Businesses get sued on the regular. Zipped lips are the order of the day.

GOLDIE: I wish I knew what to think about all this.

REAGAN: I can't tell you what to believe. But one of the first things Jay asked for when I came on board was for anti-harassment rules. He didn't want anybody in JayVision caught up. He came to me, Kesha. I didn't have to drag him to it.

(AMANDA enters.)

AMANDA: This is awfully cozy.

REAGAN: The people united will never be defeated. Here to drop these off, before I head to court.

(REAGAN hands AMANDA papers.)

GOLDIE: Wouldn't those have been easier to email?

AMANDA: We like to manage our paper trail.

REAGAN: Intellectual property needs protection.

AMANDA: Keep me posted.

(KESHA *ENTERS and waves at an exiting REGAN.*)

AMANDA: There you are. I want you sitting in on this meeting about London.

KESHA: We're taking a break from—

AMANDA: It's only twenty minutes. High time that you started learning how to handle high level negotiations.

KESHA: I'm still pretty swamped.

AMANDA: You'll get it done. The future can't be put on hold forever. It's time for us to stop kicking our priorities to the curb every time something comes up. Conference room in ten minutes.

(AMANDA *leaves.* GOLDIE *high fives* KESHA.)

GOLDIE: Way to go. Big Ben, London Bridge.

KESHA: If it weren't for her, I'd be stranded in cubicle land, trying to slash my way through a forest of peen. I'd follow her to the ends of the earth.

GOLDIE: *(Teasing)* Or the depths of hell?

KESHA: Whichever comes first.

(End Scene)

Scene 6

(Evening. REAGAN *rushes into the office. She pours herself a glass of wine and sits down at the sandbox. After she's calmed herself, she video calls* JAY.)

REAGAN: The plaintiff refused the settlement.

JAY: The fuck's the matter with her? Her "witnesses"? Discredited. Timeline shattered. Bitch needs to roll over.

REAGAN: Jay, come on. She's fifteen.

JAY: Did you try—?

REAGAN: We tripled the offer.

JAY: These donations were supposed to be the last piece.

REAGAN: I know. She's acting in bad faith, but she's fifteen.

JAY: So?

REAGAN: She might see herself as some kind of crusading heroine. Greta Thunberg—

JAY: Or our enemies might be putting her up to it.

REAGAN: Let's not get paranoid.

JAY: I'm sick of this shit. Can you nail her on breach of contract?

REAGAN: Gray area. Her age, international. The judge doesn't find you sympathetic. We have to tread carefully.

JAY: What are our options?

REAGAN: Her team telegraphed a counter offer. She wants an apology.

JAY: That's all? Done. Get her on the horn.

REAGAN: A public apology, on a major network. Iceland and here. We pay for the air time.

JAY: Fuck that bitch!!!

REAGAN: They'll put it in writing.

JAY: Well, the first deal was in writing, too.

(Beat)

REAGAN: Mitigating circumstances—

JAY: Circumstances?

REAGAN: If we want to win, we might have to humble ourselves this time.

JAY: She wants me to go on TV to say I'm something less than an animal. Not doing it. Video's forever. My children are going to be able to see that.

REAGAN: I understand.

JAY: No, you don't. You don't have kids. I need you to pull some kind of legal trick out of the hat.

REAGAN: Hat's empty.

JAY: How? She's never disputed the sex was consensual. She ran crying to mama when things weren't to her liking. Mom signs Iceland up to grab a pound of my flesh. You know what this? This is state violence.

REAGAN: If we buy the ad time, we can control when it's shown.

JAY: It'll be on the internet forever. What did she think the code words were for? Am I supposed to make my lovers sign a release now?

REAGAN: Lover isn't the right word to use in this context. Is issuing an apology...?

JAY: I won't do it. We need to go on the offensive.

REAGAN: How?

JAY: I hate to even think of it. I don't want to attack her. I'm not a bully. But she's left us no choice. I think you know what has to happen.

REAGAN: I won't initiate anything on my own. You have to provide instruction.

JAY: Wily Reagan. Start with the judge. Find a way to wring some concessions from her. My understanding is she's passionate about homeless youth.

REAGAN: I'll get Kesha on that.

JAY: Use Goldie. Time to break her in.

REAGAN: Do you want to risk that?

JAY: No time like the present.

(REAGAN *nods.*)

JAY: Make sure the court's got a more than complete picture of the evidence. Drown them in motions and discovery. That's your duty as an officer of the court.

REAGAN: Agreed.

JAY: Flood the portals with our truths.

(REAGAN *exits.* JAY *hops on the surfboard. Monitors show clear skies.*)

(*End Scene*)

Scene 7

(AMANDA *addresses* REAGAN, GOLDIE *and* KESHA.)

AMANDA: That's the plan.

GOLDIE: I feel like I still don't have a complete picture.

REAGAN: Neither do we. Better that way.

AMANDA: Enough. (*To* GOLDIE) Do you trust us?

GOLDIE: Of course. I'd feel better if I understood the scope.

AMANDA: I've told you all I can. Jay specifically requested your participation. But it's your choice.

GOLDIE: I'm in.

AMANDA: Then it's time to start the machine.

GOLDIE: Should we wait for Jay?

KESHA: This is on us.

(*Lights out*)

AMANDA: I'll take relationship management.

REAGAN: Law and investigation.

KESHA: Media strategy.

AMANDA: *(To* GOLDIE*)* We'll send you feedback. You'll crunch the numbers and determine possibilities.

GOLDIE: Run a regression?

AMANDA: If that's what it called. You'd know better than I would. *(Beat)* **Begin.**

(Black out. Powerful machine sounds)

AMANDA: Pivot!

(The women move across the stage like a machine.)

AMANDA: Step left.

REAGAN: Danger. Hold.

(They pause.)

AMANDA: Are we clear?

REAGAN: Continue, cautiously.

AMANDA: No time. Let's move.

(They march off stage.)

AMANDA: *(OS)* Wire taps.

KESHA: *(OS)* Cell phone photos.

GOLDIE: Crunch. Favorables stable.

AMANDA: Harder.

GOLDIE: Favorables falling.

(The machine begins sputtering. Bitter smoke and confusion.)

AMANDA: Fuck! Is everyone okay?

KESHA: We're screwed.

REAGAN: Maybe I can get it to.

(A popping sound)

REAGAN: No.

KESHA: Maybe we should just take the loss on this for once.

REAGAN: The strategy's beached. We don't give up. We find another way.

(Ominous machine grinding noises)

GOLDIE: What's happening? I'm scared.

KESHA: Maybe

REAGAN: Don't be scared. Get effective.

(Crash! Silence)

KESHA: *(To* AMANDA*)* What now?

AMANDA: I'm not sure which way to go.

(Ping! Light up. JAY *enters from the pool.)*

AMANDA: You shouldn't—

KESHA: We're not going to make it without him.

*(*JAY'*s package emits a beam of light that quickly illuminates the theater space and the images on the monitors.)*

GOLDIE: This is the zone.

JAY: Damn straight. *(He looks around and finds a gap in the light.)* Forward! *(He opens his arms wide to* KESHA*.)*

JAY: Come.

*(*KESHA *goes in for the hug.* JAY *gives her a slight, but noticeable hump.)*

KESHA: No.

REAGAN: Jay! Jesus Christ.

JAY: Just funning.

KESHA: You didn't tell me the whole truth, did you?

AMANDA: What's your problem?

KESHA: The last time this happened…Allison.

JAY: Something on your mind? Out with it.

KESHA: I just don't think this should be a celebration. Let's take the win and move on.

JAY: Well, I think a celebration's called for. Why don't you call her? I'm sure she'd say the same. She's a woman who knows what side her bread's buttered on.

AMANDA: I know this has been difficult, but good work.

KESHA: You've got it. *(She exits.)*

GOLDIE: Kesha!

AMANDA: Let her go.

REAGAN: You sure about that?

JAY: Of course she'll be back. I'll make sure of it. *(He whistles.)* Forward, march.

(JAY leads the women off stage.)

(End Scene)

Scene 8

(AMANDA, REAGAN, and GOLDIE work. JAY enters and holds up the settlement agreement. The women stand in a kind of reverence.)

JAY: Final nail in the coffin. It's over.

(The monitors flicker on. A bold headline: "Disgraced and discredited, Helmi Lassen retracts." The women applaud.)

JAY: Where's Kesha? She should be here for this.

AMANDA: Not back yet.

GOLDIE: She needs time, Mr Littleton.

JAY: Because giving her the world is so egregious? The direction is forward. I want to go public with a new initiative, fifty/fifty.

AMANDA: I haven't mentioned it yet.

JAY: Why not? It's good news.

AMANDA: The timing's not the best.

REAGAN: I agree. Legally you're in the clear.

JAY: Then what am I supposed to be afraid of?

REAGAN: Being insensitive.

AMANDA: Gloating.

JAY: Fuck that. We won. I'm not going to cower in the shadows. Get some eyeballs on all the donations we just made. That should destroy the insensitivity argument.

AMANDA: This could be serious. Walking took balls.

JAY: It's not the walking. It's the walking and staying gone.

AMANDA: We need to retain her.

JAY: So? Make it happen.

AMANDA: Roger that.

(End Scene)

Scene 9

(Early morning. AMANDA*'s at work.* KESHA *enters.)*

AMANDA: Are you back? You've been ignoring our calls.

KESHA: My head was in a bad place.

AMANDA: But you're better now?

KESHA: I'm back.

AMANDA: Then it's time for the morning meeting. Let's start with status reports.

*(*GOLDIE *and* REAGAN *enter.* AMANDA *shoots them a warning glance.)*

AMANDA: Final documents. Iceland's completely settled.

KESHA: It was an expensive victory.

REAGAN: She wanted things public. We gave her public: social media, the press. We told the truth and nothing but the truth, we all know much that can hurt.

AMANDA: I know I'm supposed to hate myself for saying this, even thinking it. I don't give a damn about this Helmi anymore. I know I should, but I don't. She came after us in bad faith. We engaged.

GOLDIE: What do we do now?

AMANDA: We go on.

REAGAN: Amen to that. Iceland feels like a dream we need to put behind us. A place unreal.

KESHA: Did you ever speak to this Helmi?

REAGAN: I think I must have come across her when I was there, but I don't remember. She was a butterfly floating around the men. Not my kind of girl.

AMANDA: There were a hundred off ramps. She decided to stay on the road. It's about us now. Our wants. Our future. Does anyone disagree? Speak now or bury your doubts. *(Beat)* Kesha?

KESHA: I'm back. For keeps.

GOLDIE: Welcome back.

(End Scene)

Scene 10

(Late night. Ping)

(KESHA enters from the pool. She's dressed and drying her hair. The monitors turn on depicting Iceland's swirling waters and lights.)

(KESHA *pulls on a coverall and begins working.* AMANDA *enters.*)

AMANDA: Good to see your hands steady back on the plow. *(She reads over* KESHA′s *shoulder.)* You haven't missed a step.

KESHA: Thanks.

AMANDA: I want you in London. What will it take?

KESHA: If you promise that nothing like Iceland's going to happen on your watch.

AMANDA: You're still on that?

KESHA: I don't mean Helmi. I mean the cover up. I want to work clean.

AMANDA: So do I.

KESHA: *(Relieved)* You're not worried you've worked this way too long?

AMANDA: Why do you think I want to leave? It's why I'm so desperate. My window's closing.

KESHA: I want to believe you.

(AMANDA *rubs* KESHA′s *shoulder. It's a little too intimate.*)

AMANDA: Never again.
You have my word.

KESHA: I want to believe you, but you can't just manufacture trust out of air. It's going to take time.

AMANDA: Is our trust broken?

KESHA: Not completely.

AMANDA: Let me prove myself to you. *(She undoes her own top.)* Would you be willing?

KESHA: Consent's sexy as fuck.

(KESHA *kisses* AMANDA. AMANDA *undoes* KESHA′s *blouse.*)

AMANDA: No bearing on your standing here at all.

(KESHA *laughs.*)

KESHA: I know what's in my NDA.

AMANDA: We're as free as we want to be.

KESHA: I don't know how much freedom I want.

(AMANDA *kneels, growls and puts her head in* KESHA's *crotch.*)

KESHA: Slow down. We have time.

AMANDA: I'm hungry. I'm not ashamed of it.

(JAY *enters and taps* AMANDA *on the shoulder.*)

AMANDA: Kesha?

KESHA: *(To* JAY*)* As long as you don't penetrate—

JAY: *(To* AMANDA*)* The breaking.

(JAY *takes* AMANDA's *hand.*)

JAY: *(To* AMANDA*)* Are you back?

(AMANDA *nods as* KESHA *replies…*)

KESHA: What? Yes?

AMANDA: Everything's going to be okay.

(AMANDA *puts her hand over* KESHA's *mouth.* AMANDA *and* JAY *violently sandwich* KESHA.)

(*Black out*)

(*End Scene*)

Scene 11

(KESHA *lays between* AMANDA *and* JAY, *covered by the sweater we saw earlier. All are partially dressed.* JAY *offers* AMANDA *a cigarette. She turns away.*)

AMANDA: Why aren't you completely disgusted with yourself?

JAY: You're not angry with me. You're angry this still fills you with pleasure. I want to do it again.

AMANDA: In what universe do you think that works?

JAY: There's something about her.

AMANDA: I'm going straight to London with Lotty. Bill can send us our things.

JAY: You can't do it.

AMANDA: I guess we'll see. (*She examines* KESHA.)

JAY: Still out?

AMANDA: I don't want to wake her. I'm not sure what's going to happen. This did something to me.

(KESHA *struggles to regain consciousness as* GOLDIE *and* REAGAN *enter.* JAY *rushes to the rooftop pool. Ping!* KESHA *screams from shame, pain, hurt, then collapses.*)

GOLDIE: Kesha! What's going on? She needs help. (*To* AMANDA) Why don't you help?

AMANDA: Let's get her cleaned up.

(AMANDA *reaches for* KESHA *who scrambles away.*)

KESHA: …the fuck away from me cunt.

(AMANDA *scrabbles out the front door.*)

KESHA: (*To* GOLDIE *and* REAGAN) Leave.

(*They don't move.*)

KESHA: I deserve my dignity.

REAGAN: It's not our fight.

(GOLDIE *pulls away from* REAGAN *and goes to hold* KESHA. REAGAN *exits.*)

(*End Scene*)

Scene 12

(*The next morning.* KESHA *is already at work, but frazzled.* GOLDIE *enters.*)

GOLDIE: You're back.

KESHA: So are you.

GOLDIE: Are you okay?

KESHA: You really want to know?

GOLDIE: Of course.

KESHA: You didn't text or snap me to find out. If you were so concerned—

GOLDIE: I didn't want to intrude. I wasn't sure—

KESHA: I was making out with Amanda. Just fooling around. Jay came, then. I thought…I don't know what I thought we were doing.

GOLDIE: Did he…?

KESHA: They both.

GOLDIE: God. You told him no?

KESHA: The litmus test. No, not at first. I wanted to party, but things went bad fast. Amanda held me down. And she—

GOLDIE: She would've protected you.

KESHA: I see it so clearly now. She's been grooming me for this for a long time. And I've been playing along. The sex.

GOLDIE: It was an assault.

KESHA: There are grays. It didn't start out unpleasant. I'm not hurt. But what hurts so bad is I was so fucking stupid.

GOLDIE: Don't talk about yourself that way.

KESHA: Yes, "run from trouble" Goldie.

GOLDIE: I didn't know what to do or how to react.

KESHA: Before things were always so murky. A woman I couldn't imagine myself being. Circumstances I would know better than to put myself in.

GOLDIE: But now that it's happened to you...

KESHA: It was my mistake. I'll deal with it.

GOLDIE: I don't see how you can keep working here.

KESHA: I walk and they'll screw me like we've screwed everybody else.

GOLDIE: No. Allison—

KESHA: Allison makes half of what she was making, her mother's sick and her husband's not working.

GOLDIE: There must be a way.

KESHA: Goldie, the world's not kind. It damn sure doesn't have wide open arms for me.

GOLDIE: No—

KESHA: Yes. I know who I am and what my prospects are.

GOLDIE: That's not fair.

(AMANDA *and* REAGAN *enter.*)

AMANDA: Time for the morning meeting. Anything to report?

REAGAN: I've been—

KESHA: Let me slay the elephant in the room. Now that Iceland's done. I'm back to work on the Allianz deal, not London.

(AMANDA *nods*.)

GOLDIE: This is insane. I'm not going to sit here and act like nothing's happened. What happened between you two has to get ironed out.

REAGAN: Careful.

GOLDIE: I've been careful. I'm beginning to think that's the same thing as walking myself into a ditch.

KESHA: Now you find your courage?

AMANDA: Is there a problem?

(*Beat*)

KESHA: There's not.

GOLDIE: Doing the right thing's still an option for me.

REAGAN: Your NDA.

GOLDIE: I've read it. (*She leaves.*)

REAGAN: Do you want me to—?

AMANDA: Not yet.

REAGAN: She may not know much. But we can't take the risk.

AMANDA: I'll handle it.

(REAGAN *and* AMANDA *leave*.)

(*End Scene*)

Scene 13

(*The next day.* AMANDA *welcomes* VIK *to the office*.)

AMANDA: Welcome, Mr Abdella.

VIK: Ms Stirling.

AMANDA: Chai?

VIK: Yes, please. I like that you don't say chai tea. It's like saying tea tea.

AMANDA: I've visited your country. Beautiful place. Ruthless, but beautiful.

(AMANDA *serves them.*)

AMANDA: I'm so glad you could come on such short notice. The town car was comfortable?

VIK: Very much so.

AMANDA: Goldie's such a treasure to us. I like to attack problems before they grow beyond repair.

VIK: I assure you. Goldie wasn't raised to make trouble. But this e-mail she sent you.

AMANDA: It's been a difficult time, but with these threats—

VIK: I support you one hundred percent.

AMANDA: I'm glad you're taking a firm position. Important in these days and times. And rare.

(GOLDIE *enters.*)

GOLDIE: Father?

AMANDA: I invited him.

VIK: You're to withdraw these complaints at once.

GOLDIE: What? No.

VIK: Yes. Your mother and I expect a report tonight. (*He leaves.*)

AMANDA: This was for your own good.

GOLDIE: You consider this a favor?

AMANDA: We're in a difficult situation. Consider what your father said.

GOLDIE: Do you have any idea what you've done? In the past, he has struck me for less than this.

AMANDA: You have choices. None of us are living for ourselves alone. Your father can't go back to India. There's nothing there for him. You're the hope of your family.

(GOLDIE *gives* AMANDA *the finger.*)

AMANDA: You're behaving like a child. Go. Come back when you've come to your senses.

(AMANDA *pushes* GOLDIE *from the office and locks the door.* JAY *appears on the monitors. He nods his approval.*)

(*End Scene*)

Scene 14

(JAY *waits for* AMANDA. *She enters.* JAY *holds out plane tickets.*)

JAY: Tickets to London.

AMANDA: I don't know what to say.

JAY: Take them.

(AMANDA *struggles to do so.* JAY *grabs her hand.*)

JAY: See? You thought I didn't want you anymore.

AMANDA: Please let me go.

(JAY *nuzzles* AMANDA.)

JAY: I unlocked something in you. But it was already there.

AMANDA: My daughter—

JAY: For once in your life, tell the goddamn truth.

AMANDA: Fingering Kesha, her tightness made me shiver. Then I thought of Charlotte. It made me sick.

But I couldn't stop. I didn't want to stop. Those two things can't be in my brain at the same time.

JAY: But they are. Let yourself—

AMANDA: No!

JAY: It's not wrong to have hungers.

AMANDA: I promised myself that when my baby came of age—

AMANDA: No. It's sick.

JAY: Not when we do it.

(The light beams from JAY again. Like a sun god, he pulls her down and encircles her like a snake swallowing a snake until we can't tell the difference between them.)

(Lights fade.)

(End Scene)

Scene 15

(The next morning at dawn. JAY lies on the floor snoring. AMANDA enters. She examines him carefully, then hops on his desk and "surfs".)

AMANDA: Everything's so much clearer here. *(She breathes in deeply.)* I'm soaring. Shit, I'm in the zone. I'm in it. All this time, I'm thinking... All the zone is, is a height change. *(She hops back down to stare at JAY.)*

AMANDA: You're just an ordinary man. I'm going to the pool. I'm baptizing myself into a new life.

(The WOMEN speak from the darkened monitors.)

WOMAN 1: *(OS)* You've passed the point where you can cleanse with water.

WOMAN 2: *(OS)* Flee while you still can!

AMANDA: Soon. I'm free. I can leave whenever I want.

(The monitors turn on. KESHA, GOLDIE *and* REAGAN *can finally be fully seen on screen. They hold grimy, dripping rags, mops, brooms.* AMANDA's *phone pings.)*

GOLDIE: *(OS)* It's your daughter. You going to take it.

*(*AMANDA *puts the phone down and backs away from it.)*

AMANDA: I can't talk to her right now.

GOLDIE: *(OS)* Why? Too much to handle.

AMANDA: You know why.

KESHA: *(OS)* How can you ever face her again?

AMANDA: *(To* KESHA*)* Don't you dare pressure me. I made you.

KESHA: *(OS)* Then unmade me.

REAGAN: *(OS)* Don't give her that power. We came here fully formed.

KESHA: *(OS)* Maybe you did. I see now that I was lost. Looking for a mother and lover and…

AMANDA: I helped you.

GOLDIE: *(OS)* While you helped yourself—

AMANDA: To nothing. Look in the mirror. You gave yourselves freely. There's been an exchange. Unspoken understandings. Where's the gratitude? I'm only a midwife. A mentor to you and countless others including you, Reagan. You'll never admit it, but you learned things from me. All that polish without the kill instinct is worse than useless. You got that from me.

REAGAN: *(OS)* Together we've cleaned this place many times. JayVision's the better for it. You're the better for it. Protected, richer. More impactful. We can do it again. Here. In London.

*(*AMANDA *holds out a hand to* KESHA*.)*

KESHA: *(OS)* No.

AMANDA: You don't tell me "No".

KESHA: *(OS)* I've earned that.

REAGAN: *(OS)* We cleaned up the mess, but we never cleaned what's inside you and Jay.

GOLDIE: (OS) Mess? We're talking about another woman.

AMANDA: You don't get it. Those women made themselves expendable. If you want safety from men, you align yourself with one. That's what we've all done, JayVision's given us purpose, identity, belonging, safety—

KESHA: *(OS)* No more. I loved you, Amanda. So much. As a mother, a leader, a woman.

AMANDA: You love me still. Trust me. Come with me to London.

KESHA: *(OS)* You're not going to London.

AMANDA: I am.

(JAY *awakens.*)

JAY: *(Sniffs)* Mandy?

GOLDIE: *(OS)* Amanda?

(JAY *stands and lets his beam loose.*)

KESHA & REAGAN: *(OS)* Don't.

(AMANDA's *beam emerges, the twin to* JAY's. *The beams combine as they embrace. The monitors white out.*)

(Black out)

(End Scene)

(End ACT TWO)

END OF PLAY